ESSAYS ON CONTEMPORARY EVENTS
THE PSYCHOLOGY OF NAZISM

from

The Collected Works of C. G. Jung

VOLUMES 10, 16

BOLLINGEN SERIES XX

ESSAYS ON CONTEMPORARY EVENTS

THE PSYCHOLOGY OF NAZISM

C. G. JUNG

TRANSLATED BY R.F.C. HULL

BOLLINGEN SERIES

PRINCETON UNIVERSITY PRESS

These essays were first collected in *Aufsätze zur Zeitgeschichte* (Zurich: Rascher & Cie., 1946); they were translated by Mary Briner, Barbara Hannah, and Elizabeth Welsh, and published as *Essays on Contemporary Events* (London: Kegan Paul, Trench, Trubner, 1947). The present version contains the translations by R. F. C. Hull extracted from the Collected Works: "Psychotherapy Today" and "Psychotherapy and a Philosophy of Life" are from Volume 16, © 1954, 1966 by Princeton University Press; "Wotan," "After the Catastrophe," and "Epilogue," are from Volume 10, copyright © 1964, 1970 by Princeton University Press. The introduction by Andrew Samuels is © Andrew Samuels 1988 The collection of essays in this translation was first published in 1988 in the United Kingdom by ARK PAPERBACKS, an imprint of Routledge. The illustration on the cover is a reproduction of George Grosz's painting, *The Pillars of Society*, © Estate of George Grosz/VAGA New York 1988; it is reprinted here by arrangement with the estate.

PRINTED IN THE UNITED STATES OF AMERICA BY PRINCETON
UNIVERSITY PRESS, 41 WILLIAM STREET, PRINCETON,
NEW JERSEY 08540
PUBLISHED BY PRINCETON UNIVERSITY PRESS
ALL RIGHTS RESERVED

Library of Congress Cataloging-in-Publication Data

Jung, C. G. (Carl Gustav), 1875-1961.
    [Aufsätze zur Zeitgeschichte. English]
    Essays on contemporary events / C. G. Jung ; translated by R. F. C. Hull.
        p.   cm. — (Bollingen series)
    Translation of: Aufsätze zur Zeitgeschichte.
    These translations originally published in vols. 10 (© 1954) and 16 (©
1964) of the Collected Works of C. G. Jung.
    Includes index.
    ISBN 0-691-01877-4
    1. Psychotherapy.   I. Title.   II. Series.
RC480.5.J8613   1989
150.19'54—dc19   89-30658

First Princeton/Bollingen Paperback printing, 1989

Contents

FOREWORD

By Andrew Samuels

'Well, I slipped up', said Jung to Rabbi Leo Baeck when they met in Zürich in 1946 for the first time since the Second World War (Jaffé 1971: 97–8). Jung was referring to the pre-war events surrounding his taking on of the Presidency of the General Medical Society for Psychotherapy in 1933, an international professional body nevertheless based in Germany, dominated by Germans and, at that time, coming gradually under Nazi control. Further, Jung's papers of the period, dwelling on questions of differing racial psychologies and containing generalizations about Jewish culture and psychology, seemed then and later to be, at the very least, misguidedly published. For they could easily be misunderstood as supporting Nazi racial ideology.

For instance, Jews are said 'never to have created a cultural form of their own', but rather to need a 'host nation' for their development (1934). The implication of 'Jew as parasite' follows on easily. Similarly, Jews are referred to as 'physically weaker' than others, like women in relation to men (ibid.). Therefore they have developed subtle and indirect techniques of attacking other peoples (again, according to Jung, like women attack men!).

Jung's vigorous defence of his actions and protests over the real meaning of what he wrote have been buttressed from various quarters. Indeed, given the strength of negative feeling about his conduct, if such defence had not been forthcoming, the destruction of Jung's reputation might have been the result (cf. Harms 1946). Briefly, it can be shown that Jung did his best to protect the rights of Jewish psychotherapists by altering the constitution of the GMSP so that it became a fully and formally international body with membership units composed of national societies and a special category of individual membership. Thus Jews, barred from the German national society, could retain their membership in the individual section.

Jung was also editor of the *Zentralblatt*, the Society's scientific journal. This was, to some extent, a *pro forma* appointment and Jung was geographically distant from the editorial offices. Therefore it is possible, or even likely, that he did not know of the pro-Nazi statement of principles which was inserted in the *Zentralblatt* by Professor Göring (a cousin of the Reichsmarschall) who had been made President of the (dominant) German section of the Society.

On a personal level, Jung never displayed features of anti-semitism. Many Jewish analysts studied under him, he performed numerous and risky acts of personal kindness to Jews during the war and, once the global negativism of National Socialism was apparent, he lent his pen and voice to its condemnation (Adler, personal communication, 1984).

And yet the shadow on Jung's reputation and thought remains. 'Shadow' is the apt word to use here, for it is one of the key conceptual terms in analytical psychology. The shadow, wrote Jung, is 'the thing a person has no wish to be' and yet, in some way, is (1946: para. 470). In other words, there is a negative side to every personality, his own included. One could go on to say, as Jung did, that for anything or anyone to have substance and worth, he, she or it would just have to possess a shadow. Crucial to the psychological processes brought into being by the shadow is its *integration* – not a harsh super-ego-led judgement of oneself, more a process of increased consciousness leading to self-acceptance and forgiveness.

It is my belief that this slim volume, published in German right after the war in 1946, represents a part of Jung's own attempt to integrate his personal shadow by pointing out (to himself?) that there is more to him and to his ideas than his detractors can admit.

How successfully does Jung negotiate his own shadow processes? An answer to this question must couple the speculations of psychobiography with a teasing out and objective assessment of Jung's conceptual and intellectual apparatus – that which he brought to bear in his engagement with the momentous events of the 1930s and 1940s. (We should not forget that there is a link between personality and thought, even when we distinguish them.)

That Jung had desires for leadership and behaved like the leader of a movement is still a contentious claim to make in analytical psychology. Indeed, the power aspects of the break between Freud and Jung are downplayed by both 'sides'. Jung was emphatic that he had no designs (like Freud's) to be a leader, was not interested in forming a band of 'Jungians', in spreading his ideas, or being active in the training of analysts. As I have tried to show elsewhere (1985), Jung displayed many of the features of a leader, sometimes maintaining his rule by dividing his followers, selecting individuals for special support, encouragement and advancement (often by writing Forewords for their books), and laying down rather tough criteria for the professional training of analysts. I concluded that Jung flattered his followers by maintaining that he did not want disciples; therefore no one who was involved with Jung could possibly be a mere disciple. It could be said that Jung relegated his leadership impulses and fantasies to his shadow. If so, then we may sense something psychological and personal to Jung in his keen interest in Hitler and the associated issues.

But we need more evidence before we talk glibly of Hitler as a shadow figure for Jung (that is, serving the function of carrying safely something about himself that Jung would rather not know). In the late 1930s, Jung was a prime mover in the drawing up of a list of propositions concerning the theory and practice of psychotherapy. The 'Fourteen Points', also known as 'Views Held in Common' (1938, par. 1072), were an attempt to *unify* the depth psychologies. We can see now that the seemingly inherent tendency of depth psychology to fragment made this a forlorn hope, practically speaking. But what are we to make of the use of a catch-phrase dating from the time of the formation of the League of Nations to characterize this effort? There is little doubt that Jung regarded his approach to analysis as *subsuming* those of Freud and Adler (e.g. 1929). Thus any 'Jungian' analysis would include the relevant features of an analysis of each of the other schools (though a stage of analysis known as 'transformation' was said only to be possible under the aegis of Jung's own approach).

Before all this is dismissed as grossly inflated fantasy on Jung's part, we should recall the idea that shadow and worthwhile substance are intimately linked. Alongside Jung's 'leadership complex', there is to be found a recognition of the value of other people's points of view and even a positive evaluation of disagreement and dissent: 'agreement would only spell one-sidedness and desiccation'. We need many theories before we get 'even a rough picture of the psyche's complexity' (1945: para. 198).

We have been looking at some of the personal factors which led to Jung's 'slipping up' and, in particular, perhaps, to his expectation that the leadership offered to Germany by the Nazis could develop into something positive, a kind of awakening of German potential locked up in the 'German unconscious' (1934). This leads us to the next task, which is to assess the concepts and ideas which Jung employed.

The focus has to be on questions of racial psychology and the existence of a 'racial unconscious'. Jung's assumption that there are such things was, of course, consensual for the time. Jung's thinking is extremely difficult to follow, seemingly full of contradictions. If there is such a thing as a 'collective unconscious', meaning a level in the psyche which is common to all, then surely we would expect to see far greater homogeneity in human cultures than is in fact the case? In other words, does not the idea of racial psychology contradict that of the collective unconscious?

This would undoubtedly be the case if the evidence for and phenomenology of the collective unconscious is restricted to cultural forms and patterns: religion, family and kinship organisation, economic and social structure, etc. But this level of human ideation and performance is already far removed from what Jung usually means by 'collective'. (Though the fact that there any similarities at all may be taken as evidence for the collective level coming through, as it were.) The truly collective aspect of the human psyche, which is what Jung refers to as the 'archetypes', is at one and the same time far deeper than the cultural manifestations just listed – and far more difficult to depict in words. For the level of archetype touches the psychosomatic bases of being human. Crucial to Jung's thought is the notion of the 'psychoid' layer of the unconscious: the most fundamental level which has properties in common with the organic world generally. The psychological and physiological worlds may be seen as two sides of a single coin. Thus, the psychoid nature of archetypes makes them the psychological equivalent of biological instincts. Hence the justification for the term 'collective'. (A further more technical point is that the

archetypes are indeed invisible, being only hypothetical structures; all we can experience is the manifestations of the
archetypes.)

Having established the difference between the collective and
the racial unconscious, we may now consider the value and truth
of the latter idea. 'Value' and 'truth' cannot be separated when
topics like race are discussed. If Jung had recognized this he
might have indicated much more clearly which social and
political implications of his ideas met with his approval or were
in line with his thinking. I am not suggesting that ideas with
potential dangers in them should be suppressed or withheld
from publication, only that the whole context should be taken
into account.

Is it true that Jews and Germans actually function completely
differently, psychologically speaking? And is that what Jung is
claiming? My position is that such a claim is probably not
justified. *But Jung is probably not making that claim!* Here, as so
often with Jung, it is the way in which his thought was
somewhat in advance of his own time which causes the
difficulty. That is, Jung is handicapped by the means he has
available for the communication of his theories. We can discern
the seeds of a surprisingly modern attitude to race and ethnicity.

In 1928 Jung argued against the imposition of 'the spirit' of
one race upon that of another, explicitly referring both to a
judgement of a non-European culture on the basis of European
assumptions, and also to attempts by Europeans to behave as if
they were part of another culture (e.g. India) (para. 240n). Jung
is struggling to overcome a Eurocentric cast of mind. It could
not be claimed that he was entirely successful in this, given the
patent nonsense he writes about Judaism and also about so-
called 'primitives'. With regard to the latter, there is a
thoughtless conflation of (a) modern African adult with (b)
modern European infant and (c) Neolithic beings. But there is
also a deep respect for and interest in the evolution and
development of differing cultures and this is apparent in the
'Wotan' essay in this book as well as throughout Jung's
writings.

Jung got into difficulties with Jews and political commen-
tators in the first place because of his claim and belief that depth
psychologists have a duty and a competence to observe, describe
and even interpret what is happening around them, beyond the

confines of the consulting room. Jung's feeling, expressed in his own Introduction to this book, was that in treating an individual an analyst is also 'treating' the whole culture from which that individual has sprung. Once again, we see a foreshadowing of numerous post-war socio-political critiques of the myopia of psychoanalysis when it refuses to take a position in relation to the events of the day. But there is more to Jung's desire to bring psychology to bear on culture than an interest in enhancing the healing power of individual analysis. He may also be seen as applying much of the methodology of individual analysis to cultural themes, such as the rise of Nazism (cf. Stein 1985). Note: this is a different enterprise from one which crudely employs the terminology of individual psychopathology to diagnose a cultural malaise – though subtle and enlightening variants of that can be and have been attempted. The parallel to be made is more with the practice of analysis. Jung strives to get into a transference–countertransference relationship with his 'patient' (in 'Wotan', it is Germany). Just as in individual analysis, this means allowing himself to be influenced by that which he seeks to 'treat' (countertransference). He tries to understand the behaviour of the 'patient' in terms of its antecedents (transference). Finally, he attempts to raise the level of the 'patient's' consciousness so as to allow the patient to regain a degree of self-control (interpretation). Each of these facets of the clinical analysis of an individual is employed in Jung's analysis of German cultural development, without reducing a whole country to the level of an individual.

In this short Foreword there is space only to focus on what I referred to above as 'transference' – the antecedent features of German culture, its earliest roots, its infancy even. For this is what Jung does when he introduces the figure of 'Wotan'. Germany behaves thus because, at a certain level, Germany has always behaved thus. Germany's past has an influence on Germany's present and unless the past can be opened up analytically it will continue to grip and shape the present.

So, returning to the earlier question: how successfully *does* Jung negotiate his own shadow processes? Nowhere in this book does Jung explicitly say that he too was caught up in the *Zeitgeist*; that he, too, became a devotee of Wotan; that he, too, had a 'problem' about Jews. But in the Preface to the book he refers to the 'violence' of the impact of world events on the individual analyst. And in the Introduction Jung writes of the need to know that 'your worst enemy is right there in your own heart'. A definitive answer is, of course, impossible. I think Jung really did slip up, realized that, and tried to make amends.

REFERENCES

Harms, E. (1946) 'Carl Gustav Jung – Defender of Freud and the Jews: A Chapter on European Psychiatric History Under the Nazi Yoke', *Psychiatric Quarterly* (New York), April 1946.

Jaffé, A. (1971) *From the Life and Work of C.G. Jung* (Orig. 1968), translated by R.F.C. Hull, New York: Harper & Row.

Jung, C.G. (1928) *The Relations Between the Ego and the Unconscious*, in *Collected Works*, Vol. 7.

—— (1929) 'Problems of Modern Psychotherapy' in *Collected Works*, Vol. 16.

—— (1934) 'The State of Psychotherapy Today' in *Collected Works*, Vol. 10.

—— (1938) 'Presidential Address to the 10th International Medical Congress for Psychotherapy, Oxford, 1938' in *Collected Works*, Vol. 10.

—— (1945) 'Medicine and Psychotherapy' in *Collected Works*, Vol. 16.

—— (1946) 'The Psychology of the Transference' in *Collected Works*, Vol. 16.

Samuels, A. (1985) *Jung and the Post-Jungians*, London: Routledge & Kegan Paul.

Stein, M. (1985) *Jung's Treatment of Christianity: The Psychotherapy of a Religious Tradition*, Wilmetter, Illinois: Chiron Publications.

Bibliographical Note: The Collected Works of C.G. Jung, H. Read, M. Fordham, G. Adler and W. McGuire (eds), translated mainly by R.F.C. Hull, London: Routledge & Kegan Paul, and Princeton, New Jersey: Princeton University Press. Except where indicated, references are by volume and paragraph number.

Preface

Medical psychotherapy, for practical reasons, has to deal with the whole of the psyche. Therefore it is bound to come to terms with all those factors, biological as well as social and mental, which have a vital influence on psychic life.

We are living in times of great disruption: political passions are aflame, internal upheavals have brought nations to the brink of chaos, and the very foundations of our *Weltanschauung* are shattered. This critical state of things has such a tremendous influence on the psychic life of the individual that the doctor must follow its effects with more than usual attention. The storm of events does not sweep down upon him only from the great world outside; he feels the violence of its impact even in the quiet of his consulting-room and in the privacy of the medical consultation. As he has a responsibility towards his patients, he cannot afford to withdraw to the peaceful island of undisturbed scientific work, but must constantly descend into the arena of world events, in order to join in the battle of conflicting passions and opinions. Were he to remain aloof from the tumult, the calamity of his time would reach him only from afar, and his patient's suffering would find neither ear nor understanding. He would be at a loss to know how to talk to him, and to help him out of his isolation. For this reason the psychologist cannot avoid coming to grips with contemporary history, even if his very soul shrinks from the political uproar, the lying propaganda, and the jarring speeches of the demagogues. We need not mention his duties as a citizen, which confront him with a similar task. As a physician, he has a higher obligation to humanity in this respect.

From time to time, therefore, I have felt obliged to step beyond the usual bounds of my profession. The experience of the psychologist is of a rather special kind, and it seemed to me that the general public might find it useful to hear his point of view. This was hardly a far-fetched conclusion, for surely the most naïve of laymen could not fail to see that many contemporary figures and events were positively asking for psychological elucidation. Were psychopathic symptoms ever more conspicuous than in the contemporary political scene?

It has never been my wish to meddle in the political questions of the day. But in the course of the years I have written a few papers which give my reactions to current events. The present book contains a collection of these occasional essays, all written between 1936 and 1946. It is natural enough that my thoughts should have been especially concerned with Germany, which has been a problem to me ever since the first World War. My statements have evidently led to all manner of misunderstandings, which are chiefly due, no doubt, to the fact that my psychological point of view strikes many people as new and therefore strange. Instead of embarking upon lengthy arguments in an attempt to clear up these misunderstandings, I have found it simpler to collect all the passages in my other writings which deal with the same theme and to put them in an epilogue. The reader will thus be in a position to get a clear picture of the facts for himself.

1

Introduction:
the fight with the shadow[1]

The indescribable events of the last decade lead one to sus-
pect that a peculiar psychological disturbance was a possible
cause. If you ask a psychiatrist what he thinks about these things,
you must naturally expect to get an answer from his particular
point of view. Even so, as a scientist, the psychiatrist makes no
claim to omniscience, for he regards his opinion merely as one
contribution to the enormously complicated task of finding a
comprehensive explanation.

When one adopts the standpoint of psychopathology, it is not
easy to address an audience which may include people who know
nothing of this specialized and difficult field. But there is one
simple rule that you should bear in mind: the psychopathology
of the masses is rooted in the psychology of the individual.
Psychic phenomena of this class can be investigated in the individual. Only if one succeeds in establishing that certain phenomena or symptoms are common to a number of different
individuals can one begin to examine the analogous mass phenomena.

As you perhaps already know, I take account of the psychology both of the conscious and of the unconscious, and this
includes the investigation of dreams. Dreams are the natural
products of unconscious psychic activity. We have known for a
long time that there is a biological relationship between the unconscious processes and the activity of the conscious mind. This
relationship can best be described as a compensation, which

---

[1] [A broadcast talk in the Third Programme of the British Broadcasting Corporation,
on November 3, 1946. First published in *The Listener* (London), XXXVI (1946),
no. 930, 615–16.]

1

means that any deficiency in consciousness—such as exaggeration, one-sidedness, or lack of a function—is suitably supplemented by an unconscious process.

As early as 1918, I noticed peculiar disturbances in the unconscious of my German patients which could not be ascribed to their personal psychology. Such non-personal phenomena always manifest themselves in dreams as mythological motifs that are also to be found in legends and fairytales throughout the world. I have called these mythological motifs *archetypes*: that is, typical modes or forms in which these collective phenomena are experienced. There was a disturbance of the collective unconscious in every single one of my German patients. One can explain these disorders causally, but such an explanation is apt to be unsatisfactory, as it is easier to understand archetypes by their aim rather than by their causality. The archetypes I had observed expressed primitivity, violence, and cruelty. When I had seen enough of such cases, I turned my attention to the peculiar state of mind then prevailing in Germany. I could only see signs of depression and a great restlessness, but this did not allay my suspicions. In a paper which I published at that time, I suggested that the "blond beast" was stirring in an uneasy slumber and that an outburst was not impossible.[2]

This condition was not by any means a purely Teutonic phenomenon, as became evident in the following years. The onslaught of primitive forces was more or less universal. The only difference lay in the German mentality itself, which proved to be more susceptible because of the marked proneness of the Germans to mass psychology. Moreover, defeat and social disaster had increased the herd instinct in Germany, so that it became more and more probable that Germany would be the first victim among the Western nations—victim of a mass movement brought about by an upheaval of forces lying dormant in the unconscious, ready to break through all moral barriers. These forces, in accordance with the rule I have mentioned, were meant to be a compensation. If such a compensatory move of the unconscious is not integrated into consciousness in an individual, it leads to a neurosis or even to a psychosis, and the same would apply to a collectivity. Clearly there must be something

[2] Cf. "The Role of the Unconscious," in *Civilization in Transition*, par. 17.

2

wrong with the conscious attitude for a compensatory move of this kind to be possible; something must be amiss or exaggerated, because only a faulty consciousness can call forth a counter-move on the part of the unconscious. Well, innumerable things were wrong, as you know, and opinions are thoroughly divided about them. Which is the correct opinion will be learned only *ex effectu;* that is, we can only discover what the defects in the consciousness of our epoch are by observing the kind of reaction they call forth from the unconscious.

As I have already told you, the tide that rose in the unconscious after the first World War was reflected in individual dreams, in the form of collective, mythological symbols which expressed primitivity, violence, cruelty: in short, all the powers of darkness. When such symbols occur in a large number of individuals and are not understood, they begin to draw these individuals together as if by magnetic force, and thus a mob is formed. Its leader will soon be found in the individual who has the least resistance, the least sense of responsibility and, because of his inferiority, the greatest will to power. He will let loose everything that is ready to burst forth, and the mob will follow with the irresistible force of an avalanche.

I had observed the German revolution in the test-tube of the individual, so to speak, and I was fully aware of the immense dangers involved when such people crowd together. But I did not know at the time whether there were enough of them in Germany to make a general explosion inevitable. However, I was able to follow up quite a number of cases and to observe how the uprush of the dark forces deployed itself in the individual test-tube. I could watch these forces as they broke through the individual's moral and intellectual self-control, and as they flooded his conscious world. There was often terrific suffering and destruction; but when the individual was able to cling to a shred of reason, or to preserve the bonds of a human relationship, a new compensation was brought about in the unconscious by the very chaos of the conscious mind, and this compensation could be integrated into consciousness. New symbols then appeared, of a collective nature, but this time reflecting the forces of *order.* There was measure, proportion, and symmetrical arrangement in these symbols, expressed in their peculiar mathematical and geometrical structure. They represent a kind of axial system and are known as *mandalas*. I am afraid I cannot go into an explanation of these highly technical matters here, but, however incomprehensible they may sound, I must mention them in passing because they represent a gleam of hope, and we need hope very badly in this time of dissolution and chaotic disorder.

The world-wide confusion and disorder reflect a similar condition in the mind of the individual, but this lack of orientation is compensated in the unconscious by the archetypes of order. Here again I must point out that if these symbols of order are not integrated into consciousness, the forces they express will accumulate to a dangerous degree, just as the forces of destruction and disorder did twenty-five years ago. The integration of unconscious contents is an individual act of realization, of understanding, and moral evaluation. It is a most difficult task, demanding a high degree of ethical responsibility. Only relatively few individuals can be expected to be capable of such an achievement, and they are not the political but the moral leaders of mankind. The maintenance and further development of civilization depend on such individuals, for it is obvious enough that the consciousness of the masses has not advanced since the first World War. Only certain reflective minds have been enriched, and their moral and intellectual horizon has been considerably enlarged by the realization of the immense and overwhelming power of evil, and of the fact that mankind is capable of becoming merely its instrument. But the average man is still where he was at the end of the first World War. Therefore it is only too obvious that the vast majority are incapable of integrating the forces of order. On the contrary, it is even probable that these forces will encroach upon consciousness and take it by surprise and violence, against our will. We see the first symptoms everywhere: totalitarianism and State slavery. The value and importance of the individual are rapidly decreasing and the chances of his being heard will vanish more and more.

This process of deterioration will be long and painful, but I fear it is inevitable. Yet in the long run it will prove to be the only way by which man's lamentable unconsciousness, his childishness and individual weakness, can be replaced by a future man, who knows that he himself is the maker of his fate and that the State is his servant and not his master. But man will reach

4

this level only when he realizes that, through his unconsciousness, he has gambled away the fundamental *droits de l'homme*. Germany has given us a most instructive example of the psychological development in question. There the first World War released the hidden power of evil, just as the war itself was released by the accumulation of unconscious masses and their blind desires. The so-called "Friedenskaiser" was one of the first victims and, not unlike Hitler, he voiced these lawless, chaotic desires and was thus led into war, and into the inevitable catastrophe. The second World War was a repetition of the same psychic process but on an infinitely greater scale.

As I have said, the uprush of mass instincts was symptomatic of a compensatory move of the unconscious. Such a move was possible because the conscious state of the people had become estranged from the natural laws of human existence. Thanks to industrialization, large portions of the population were uprooted and were herded together in large centres. This new form of existence—with its mass psychology and social dependence on the fluctuation of markets and wages—produced an individual who was unstable, insecure, and suggestible. He was aware that his life depended on boards of directors and captains of industry, and he supposed, rightly or wrongly, that they were chiefly motivated by financial interests. He knew that, no matter how conscientiously he worked, he could still fall a victim at any moment to economic changes which were utterly beyond his control. And there was nothing else for him to rely on. Moreover, the system of moral and political education prevailing in Germany had already done its utmost to permeate everybody with a spirit of dull obedience, with the belief that every desirable thing must come from above, from those who by divine decree sat on top of the law-abiding citizen, whose feelings of personal responsibility were overruled by a rigid sense of duty. No wonder, therefore, that it was precisely Germany that fell a prey to mass psychology, though she is by no means the only nation threatened by this dangerous germ. The influence of mass psychology has spread far and wide.

The individual's feeling of weakness, indeed of non-existence, was thus compensated by the eruption of hitherto unknown desires for power. It was the revolt of the powerless, the insatiable greed of the "have-nots." By such devious means the unconscious compels man to become conscious of himself. Unfortunately, there were no values in the conscious mind of the individual which would have enabled him to understand and integrate the reaction when it reached consciousness. Nothing but materialism was preached by the highest intellectual authorities. The Churches were evidently unable to cope with this new situation; they could do nothing but protest and that did not help very much. Thus the avalanche rolled on in Germany and produced its leader, who was elected as a tool to complete the ruin of the nation. But what was his original intention? He dreamed of a "new order." We should be badly mistaken if we assumed that he did not really intend to create an international order of some kind. On the contrary, deep down in his being he was motivated by the forces of order, which became operative in him the moment desirousness and greed had taken complete possession of his conscious mind. Hitler was the exponent of a "new order," and that is the real reason why practically every German fell for him. The Germans wanted order, but they made the fatal mistake of choosing the principal victim of disorder and unchecked greed for their leader. Their individual attitude remained unchanged: just as they were greedy for power, so they were greedy for order. Like the rest of the world, they did not understand wherein Hitler's significance lay, that he symbolized something in every individual. He was the most prodigious personification of all human inferiorities. He was an utterly incapable, unadapted, irresponsible, psychopathic personality, full of empty, infantile fantasies, but cursed with the keen intuition of a rat or a guttersnipe. He represented the shadow, the inferior part of everybody's personality, in an overwhelming degree, and this was another reason why they fell for him.

But what could they have done? In Hitler, every German should have seen his own shadow, his own worst danger. It is everybody's allotted fate to become conscious of and learn to deal with this shadow. But how could the Germans be expected to understand this, when nobody in the world can understand such a simple truth? The world will never reach a state of order until this truth is generally recognized. In the meantime, we amuse ourselves by advancing all sorts of external and secondary reasons why it cannot be reached, though we know well enough that conditions depend very largely on the way we take them. If, for instance, the French Swiss should assume that the German Swiss were all devils, we in Switzerland could have the grandest civil war in no time, and we could also discover the most convincing economic reasons why such a war was inevitable. Well—we just don't, for we learned our lesson more than four hundred years ago. We came to the conclusion that it is better to avoid external wars, so we went home and took the strife with us. In Switzerland we have built up the "perfect democracy," where our warlike instincts expend themselves in the form of domestic quarrels called "political life." We fight each other within the limits of the law and the constitution, and we are inclined to think of democracy as a chronic state of mitigated civil war. We are far from being at peace with ourselves: on the contrary, we hate and fight each other because we have succeeded in introverting war. Our peaceful outward demeanour merely serves to safeguard our domestic quarrels from foreign intruders who might disturb us. Thus far we have succeeded, but we are still a long way from the ultimate goal. We still have enemies in the flesh, and we have not yet managed to introvert our political disharmonies. We still labour under the unwholesome delusion that we should be at peace within ourselves. Yet even our national, mitigated state of war would soon come to an end if everybody could see his own shadow and begin the only struggle that is really worth while: the fight against the overwhelming power-drive of the shadow. We have a tolerable social order in Switzerland because we fight among ourselves. Our order would be perfect if only everybody could direct his aggressiveness inwards, into his own psyche. Unfortunately, our religious education prevents us from doing this, with its false promises of an immediate peace within. Peace may come in the end, but only when victory and defeat have lost their meaning. What did our Lord mean when he said: "I came not to send peace, but a sword"?

To the extent that we are able to found a true democracy—a conditional fight among ourselves, either collective or individual—we realize, we make real, the factors of order, because then it becomes absolutely necessary to live in orderly circumstances. In a democracy you simply cannot afford the disturbing complications of outside interference. How can you run a

7

civil war properly when you are attacked from without? When, on the other hand, you are seriously at variance with yourself, you welcome your fellow human beings as possible sympathizers with your cause, and on this account you are disposed to be friendly and hospitable. But you politely avoid people who want to be helpful and relieve you of your troubles. We psychologists have learned, through long and painful experience, that you deprive a man of his best resource when you help him to get rid of his complexes. You can only help him to become sufficiently aware of them and to start a conscious conflict within himself. In this way the complex becomes a focus of life. Anything that disappears from your psychological inventory is apt to turn up in the guise of a hostile neighbour, who will inevitably arouse your anger and make you aggressive. It is surely better to know that your worst enemy is right there in your own heart. Man's warlike instincts are ineradicable—therefore a state of perfect peace is unthinkable. Moreover, peace is uncanny because it breeds war. True democracy is a highly psychological institution which takes account of human nature as it is and makes allowances for the necessity of conflict within its own national boundaries.

If you now compare the present state of mind of the Germans with my argument you will appreciate the enormous task with which the world is confronted. We can hardly expect the demoralized German masses to realize the import of such psychological truths, no matter how simple. But the great Western democracies have a better chance, so long as they can keep out of those wars that always tempt them to believe in external enemies and in the desirability of internal peace. The marked tendency of the Western democracies to internal dissension is the very thing that could lead them into a more hopeful path. But I am afraid that this hope will be deferred by powers which still believe in the contrary process, in the destruction of the individual and the increase of the fiction we call the State. The psychologist believes firmly in the individual as the sole carrier of mind and life. Society and the State derive their quality from the individual's mental condition, for they are made up of individuals and the way they are organized. Obvious as this fact is, it has still not permeated collective opinion sufficiently for people to refrain from using the word "State" as if it referred to a sort of super-individual endowed with inexhaustible power

8

and resourcefulness. The State is expected nowadays to accomplish what nobody would expect from an individual. The dangerous slope leading down to mass psychology begins with this plausible thinking in large numbers, in terms of powerful organizations where the individual dwindles to a mere cipher. Everything that exceeds a certain human size evokes equally inhuman powers in man's unconscious. Totalitarian demons are called forth, instead of the realization that all that can really be accomplished is an infinitesimal step forward in the moral nature of the individual. The destructive power of our weapons has increased beyond all measure, and this forces a psychological question on mankind: Is the mental and moral condition of the men who decide on the use of these weapons equal to the enormity of the possible consequences?

2

Wotan[1]

En Germanie naistront diverses sectes,
S'approchans fort de l'heureux paganisme:
Le cœur captif et petites receptes
Feront retour à payer la vraye disme.
—*Prophéties de Maistre Michel Nostradamus,* 1555

³⁷¹ When we look back to the time before 1914, we find ourselves living in a world of events which would have been incon-
ceivable before the war. We were even beginning to regard war
between civilized nations as a fable, thinking that such an ab-
surdity would become less and less possible in our rational, inter-
nationally organized world. And what came after the war was a
veritable witches' sabbath. Everywhere fantastic revolutions, violent alterations of the map, reversions in politics to medieval or
even antique prototypes, totalitarian states that engulf their
neighbours and outdo all previous theocracies in their absolutist
claims, persecutions of Christians and Jews, wholesale political
murder, and finally we have witnessed a light-hearted piratical
raid on a peaceful, half-civilized people.[2]

³⁷² With such goings on in the wide world it is not in the least

---

[1] [First published as "Wotan," *Neue Schweizer Rundschau* (Zurich), n.s., III (March, 1936), 657–69. Motto, trans. by H. C. Roberts:

"In Germany shall divers sects arise,
Coming very near to happy paganism.
The heart captivated and small receivings
Shall open the gate to pay the true tithe."]

[2] Abyssinia.

10

surprising that there should be equally curious manifestations on a smaller scale in other spheres. In the realm of philosophy we shall have to wait some time before anyone is able to assess the kind of age we are living in. But in the sphere of religion we can see at once that some very significant things have been happening. We need feel no surprise that in Russia the colourful splendours of the Eastern Orthodox Church have been superseded by the Movement of the Godless—indeed, one breathed a sigh of relief oneself when one emerged from the haze of an Orthodox church with its multitude of lamps and entered an honest mosque, where the sublime and invisible omnipresence of God was not crowded out by a superfluity of sacred paraphernalia. Tasteless and pitiably unintelligent as it is, and however deplorable the low spiritual level of the "scientific" reaction, it was inevitable that nineteenth-century "scientific" enlightenment should one day dawn in Russia.

But what is more than curious—indeed, piquant to a degree—is that an ancient god of storm and frenzy, the long quiescent Wotan, should awake, like an extinct volcano, to new activity, in a civilized country that had long been supposed to have outgrown the Middle Ages. We have seen him come to life in the German Youth Movement, and right at the beginning the blood of several sheep was shed in honour of his resurrection. Armed with rucksack and lute, blond youths, and sometimes girls as well, were to be seen as restless wanderers on every road from the North Cape to Sicily, faithful votaries of the roving god. Later, towards the end of the Weimar Republic, the wandering role was taken over by the thousands of unemployed, who were to be met with everywhere on their aimless journeys. By 1933 they wandered no longer, but marched in their hundreds of thousands. The Hitler movement literally brought the whole of Germany to its feet, from five-year-olds to veterans, and produced the spectacle of a nation migrating from one place to another. Wotan the wanderer was on the move. He could be seen, looking rather shamefaced, in the meeting-house of a sect of simple folk in North Germany, disguised as Christ sitting on a white horse. I do not know if these people were aware of Wotan's ancient connection with the figures of Christ and Dionysus, but it is not very probable.

Wotan is a restless wanderer who creates unrest and stirs up

11

strife, now here, now there, and works magic. He was soon changed by Christianity into the devil, and only lived on in fading local traditions as a ghostly hunter who was seen with his retinue, flickering like a will o' the wisp through the stormy night. In the Middle Ages the role of the restless wanderer was taken over by Ahasuerus, the Wandering Jew, which is not a Jewish but a Christian legend. The motif of the wanderer who has not accepted Christ was projected on the Jews, in the same way as we always rediscover our unconscious psychic contents in other people. At any rate the coincidence of anti-Semitism with the reawakening of Wotan is a psychological subtlety that may perhaps be worth mentioning.

The German youths who celebrated the solstice with sheep-sacrifices were not the first to hear a rustling in the primeval forest of the unconscious. They were anticipated by Nietzsche, Schuler, Stefan George, and Ludwig Klages.[3] The literary tradition of the Rhineland and the country south of the Main has a classical stamp that cannot easily be got rid of; every interpretation of intoxication and exuberance is apt to be taken back to classical models, to Dionysus, to the *puer aeternus* and the cosmogonic Eros.[4] No doubt it sounds better to academic ears to interpret these things as Dionysus, but Wotan might be a more

---

[3] Ever since Nietzsche (1844–1900) there has been consistent emphasis on the "Dionysian" aspect of life in contrast to its "Apollonian" opposite. Since "The Birth of Tragedy" (1872), the dark, earthy, feminine side, with its mantic and orgiastic characteristics, has possessed the imagination of philosophers and poets. Irrationality gradually came to be regarded as the ideal; this is found, for example, all through the research of Alfred Schuler (d. 1923) into the mystery religions, and particularly in the writings of Klages (b. 1872 [d. 1956]), who expounded the philosophy of "irrationalism." To Klages, logos and consciousness are the destroyers of creative preconscious life. In these writers we witness the origin of a gradual rejection of reality and a negation of life as it is. This leads in the end to a cult of ecstasy, culminating in the self-dissolution of consciousness in death, which meant, to them, the conquest of material limitations.

The poetry of Stefan George (1868–1933) combines elements of classical civilization, medieval Christianity, and oriental mysticism. George deliberately attacked nineteenth- and twentieth-century rationalism. His aristocratic message of mystical beauty and of an esoteric conception of history had a deep influence on German youth. His work has been exploited by unscrupulous politicians for propaganda purposes.

[4] *Vom kosmogonischen Eros* is the title of one of Klages' main works (first pub. 1922).

correct interpretation. He is the god of storm and frenzy, the unleasher of passions and the lust of battle; moreover he is a superlative magician and artist in illusion who is versed in all secrets of an occult nature

Nietzsche's case is certainly a peculiar one. He had no knowledge of Germanic literature; he discovered the "cultural Philistine"; and the announcement that "God is dead" led to Zarathustra's meeting with an unknown god in unexpected form, who approached him sometimes as an enemy and sometimes disguised as Zarathustra himself. Zarathustra, too, was a soothsayer, a magician, and the storm-wind:

> And like a wind shall I come to blow among them, and with my spirit shall take away the breath of their spirit; thus my future wills it.
> Truly, a strong wind is Zarathustra to all that are low; and this counsel gives he to his enemies and to all that spit and spew:
> "Beware of spitting against the wind." [5]

And when Zarathustra dreamed that he was guardian of the graves in the "lone mountain fortress of death," and was making a mighty effort to open the gates, suddenly

> A roaring wind tore the gates asunder; whistling, shrieking, and keening, it cast a black coffin before me.
> And amid the roaring and whistling and shrieking the coffin burst open and spouted a thousand peals of laughter.

The disciple who interpreted the dream said to Zarathustra:

> Are you not yourself the wind with shrill whistling, which bursts open the gates of the fortress of death?
> Are you not yourself the coffin filled with life's gay malice and angel-grimaces? [6]

In 1863 or 1864, in his poem "To the Unknown God," Nietzsche had written:

> I shall and will know thee, Unknown One,
> Who searchest out the depths of my soul,
> And blowest through my life like a storm,
> Ungraspable, and yet my kinsman!
> I shall and will know thee, and serve thee.

[5] *Thus Spake Zarathustra*, trans. by Kaufmann, p. 211 (mod.).
[6] Ibid., p. 247 (mod.).

Twenty years later, in his "Mistral Song," he wrote:

> Mistral wind, chaser of clouds,
> Killer of gloom, sweeper of the skies,
> Raging storm-wind, how I love thee!
> Are we not both the first-fruits
> Of the same womb, forever predestined
> To the same fate? [7]

In the dithyramb known as "Ariadne's Lament," Nietzsche is completely the victim of the hunter-god:

> Stretched out, shuddering,
> Like a half-dead thing whose feet are warmed,
> Shaken by unknown fevers,
> Shivering with piercing icy frost arrows,
> Hunted by thee, O thought,
> Unutterable! Veiled! horrible one!
> Thou huntsman behind the clouds.
> Struck down by thy lightning bolt,
> Thou mocking eye that stares at me from the dark!
> Thus I lie,
> Writhing, twisting, tormented
> With all eternal tortures,
> Smitten
> By thee, cruel huntsman,
> Thou unknown—God! [8]

This remarkable image of the hunter-god is not a mere dithyrambic figure of speech but is based on an experience which Nietzsche had when he was fifteen years old, at Pforta. It is described in a book by Nietzsche's sister, Elizabeth Foerster-Nietzsche.[9] As he was wandering about in a gloomy wood at night, he was terrified by a "blood-curdling shriek from a neighbouring lunatic asylum," and soon afterwards he came face to face with a huntsman whose "features were wild and uncanny." Setting his whistle to his lips "in a valley surrounded by wild scrub," the huntsman "blew such a shrill blast" that Nietzsche lost consciousness—but woke up again in Pforta. It was a nightmare. It is significant that in his dream Nietzsche, who in reality

---

[7] *Werke*, V, pp. 457f. and 495; trans. by R. F. C. Hull.
[8] *Thus Spake Zarathustra*, Kaufmann trans., p. 365.
[9] *Der werdende Nietzsche*, pp. 84ff.

intended to go to Eisleben, Luther's town, discussed with the huntsman the question of going instead to "Teutschenthal" (Valley of the Germans). No one with ears to hear can misunderstand the shrill whistling of the storm-god in the nocturnal wood.

Was it really only the classical philologist in Nietzsche that led to the god being called Dionysus instead of Wotan—or was it perhaps due to his fateful meeting with Wagner?

In his *Reich ohne Raum,* which was first published in 1919, Bruno Goetz saw the secret of coming events in Germany in the form of a very strange vision. I have never forgotten this little book, for it struck me at the time as a forecast of the German weather. It anticipates the conflict between the realm of ideas and life, between Wotan's dual nature as a god of storm and a god of secret musings. Wotan disappeared when his oaks fell and appeared again when the Christian God proved too weak to save Christendom from fratricidal slaughter. When the Holy Father at Rome could only impotently lament before God the fate of the *grex segregatus,* the one-eyed old hunter, on the edge of the German forest, laughed and saddled Sleipnir.

We are always convinced that the modern world is a reasonable world, basing our opinion on economic, political, and psychological factors. But if we may forget for a moment that we are living in the year of Our Lord 1936, and, laying aside our well-meaning, all-too-human reasonableness, may burden God or the gods with the responsibility for contemporary events instead of man, we would find Wotan quite suitable as a causal hypothesis. In fact I venture the heretical suggestion that the unfathomable depths of Wotan's character explain more of National Socialism than all three reasonable factors put together. There is no doubt that each of these factors explains an important aspect of what is going on in Germany, but Wotan explains yet more. He is particularly enlightening in regard to a general phenomenon which is so strange to anybody not a German that it remains incomprehensible even after the deepest reflection.

Perhaps we may sum up this general phenomenon as *Ergriffenheit*—a state of being seized or possessed. The term postulates not only an *Ergriffener* (one who is seized) but also an *Ergreifer* (one who seizes). Wotan is an *Ergreifer* of men, and, unless one

15

wishes to deify Hitler—which has indeed actually happened—he is really the only explanation. It is true that Wotan shares this quality with his cousin Dionysus, but Dionysus seems to have exercised his influence mainly on women. The maenads were a species of female storm-troopers, and, according to mythical reports, were dangerous enough. Wotan confined himself to the berserkers, who found their vocation as the Blackshirts of mythical kings.

A mind that is still childish thinks of the gods as metaphysical entities existing in their own right, or else regards them as playful or superstitious inventions. From either point of view the parallel between Wotan *redivivus* and the social, political, and psychic storm that is shaking Germany might have at least the value of a parable. But since the gods are without doubt personifications of psychic forces, to assert their metaphysical existence is as much an intellectual presumption as the opinion that they could ever be invented. Not that "psychic forces" have anything to do with the conscious mind, fond as we are of playing with the idea that consciousness and psyche are identical. This is only another piece of intellectual presumption. "Psychic forces" have far more to do with the realm of the unconscious. Our mania for rational explanations obviously has its roots in our fear of metaphysics, for the two were always hostile brothers. Hence anything unexpected that approaches us from that dark realm is regarded either as coming from outside and therefore as real, or else as an hallucination and therefore not true. The idea that anything could be real or true which does *not* come from outside has hardly begun to dawn on contemporary man.

For the sake of better understanding and to avoid prejudice, we could of course dispense with the name "Wotan" and speak instead of the *furor teutonicus*. But we should only be saying the same thing and not as well, for the *furor* in this case is a mere psychologizing of Wotan and tells us no more than that the Germans are in a state of "fury." We thus lose sight of the most peculiar feature of this whole phenomenon, namely, the dramatic aspect of the *Ergreifer* and the *Ergriffener*. The impressive thing about the German phenomenon is that one man, who is obviously "possessed," has infected a whole nation to such an extent that everything is set in motion and has started rolling on its course towards perdition.

16

It seems to me that Wotan hits the mark as an hypothesis. Apparently he really was only asleep in the Kyffhäuser mountain until the ravens called him and announced the break of day. He is a fundamental attribute of the German psyche, an irrational psychic factor which acts on the high pressure of civilization like a cyclone and blows it away. Despite their crankiness, the Wotan-worshippers seem to have judged things more correctly than the worshippers of reason. Apparently everyone had forgotten that Wotan is a Germanic datum of first importance, the truest expression and unsurpassed personification of a fundamental quality that is particularly characteristic of the Germans. Houston Stewart Chamberlain is a symptom which arouses suspicion that other veiled gods may be sleeping elsewhere. The emphasis on the Germanic race (vulgarly called "Aryan"), the Germanic heritage, blood and soil, the Wagalaweia songs,[10] the ride of the Valkyries, Jesus as a blond and blue-eyed hero, the Greek mother of St. Paul, the devil as an international Alberich in Jewish or Masonic guise, the Nordic aurora borealis as the light of civilization, the inferior Mediterranean races—all this is the indispensable scenery for the drama that is taking place and at bottom they all mean the same thing: a god has taken possession of the Germans and their house is filled with a "mighty rushing wind." It was soon after Hitler seized power, if I am not mistaken, that a cartoon appeared in *Punch* of a raving berserker tearing himself free from his bonds. A hurricane has broken loose in Germany while we still believe it is fine weather.

Things are comparatively quiet in Switzerland, though occasionally there is a puff of wind from the north or south. Sometimes it has a slightly ominous sound, sometimes it whispers so harmlessly or even idealistically that no one is alarmed. "Let sleeping dogs lie"—we manage to get along pretty well with this proverbial wisdom. It is sometimes said that the Swiss are singularly averse to making a problem of themselves. I must rebut this accusation: the Swiss do have their problems but they would not admit it for anything in the world, even though they see which way the wind is blowing. We thus pay our tribute to the time

10 [After the meaningless refrains sung by the Rhine maidens in Wagner's *Ring* cycle: "*Weia! Waga! Wagala weia!*," etc.—EDITORS.]

17

of storm and stress in Germany, but we never mention it, and this enables us to feel vastly superior.

It is above all the Germans who have an opportunity, perhaps unique in history, to look into their own hearts and to learn what those perils of the soul were from which Christianity tried to rescue mankind. Germany is a land of spiritual catastrophes, where nature never makes more than a pretence of peace with world-ruling reason. The disturber of the peace is a wind that blows into Europe from Asia's vastness, sweeping in on a wide front from Thrace to the Baltic, scattering the nations before it like dry leaves, or inspiring thoughts that shake the world to its foundations. It is an elemental Dionysus breaking into the Apollonian order. The rouser of this tempest is named Wotan, and we can learn a good deal about him from the political confusion and spiritual upheaval he has caused throughout history. For a more exact investigation of his character, however, we must go back to the age of myths, which did not explain everything in terms of man and his limited capacities but sought the deeper cause in the psyche and its autonomous powers. Man's earliest intuitions personified these powers as gods, and described them in the myths with great care and circumstantiality according to their various characters. This could be done the more readily on account of the firmly established primordial types or images which are innate in the unconscious of many races and exercise a direct influence upon them. Because the behaviour of a race takes on its specific character from its underlying images we can speak of an archetype "Wotan." [11] As an autonomous psychic factor, Wotan produces effects in the collective life of a people and thereby reveals his own nature. For Wotan has a peculiar biology of his own, quite apart from the nature of man. It is only from time to time that individuals fall under the irresistible influence of this unconscious factor. When it is quiescent, one is no more aware of the archetype Wotan than of a latent epilepsy. Could the Germans who were adults in 1914 have foreseen what they would be today? Such amazing transformations are the effect of the god of wind, that "bloweth where it listeth, and thou hearest the sound thereof, but canst

[11] One should read what Bruno Goetz (*Deutsche Dichtung*, pp. 36ff. and 72ff.) has to say about Odin as the German wanderer-god. Unfortunately I only read this book after I had finished my article.

not tell whence it cometh, nor whither it goeth." It seizes everything in its path and overthrows everything that is not firmly
rooted. When the wind blows it shakes everything that is insecure, whether without or within.

Martin Ninck has recently published a monograph [12] which
is a most welcome addition to our knowledge of Wotan's nature.
The reader need not fear that this book is nothing but a scientific study written with academic aloofness from the subject.
Certainly the right to scientific objectivity is fully preserved, and
the material has been collected with extraordinary thoroughness
and presented in unusually clear form. But over and above all
this one feels that the author is vitally interested in it, that the
chord of Wotan is vibrating in him too. This is no criticism—on
the contrary it is one of the chief merits of the book, which without this enthusiasm might easily have degenerated into a tedious
catalogue.

Ninck sketches a really magnificent portrait of the German
archetype Wotan. He describes him in ten chapters, using all the
available sources, as the berserker, the god of storm, the wanderer, the warrior, the *Wunsch-* and *Minne*-god, the lord of
the dead and of the *Einherier*,[13] the master of secret knowledge,
the magician, and the god of the poets. Neither the Valkyries
nor the *Fylgja*[14] are forgotten, for they form part of the mythological background and fateful significance of Wotan. Ninck's
inquiry into the name and its origin is particularly instructive.
He shows that Wotan is not only a god of rage and frenzy who
embodies the instinctual and emotional aspect of the unconscious. Its intuitive and inspiring side also manifests itself in
him, for he understands the runes and can interpret fate.

The Romans identified Wotan with Mercury, but his character does not really correspond to any Roman or Greek god,
although there are certain resemblances. He is a wanderer like
Mercury, for instance, rules over the dead like Pluto and Kronos,
and is connected with Dionysus by his emotional frenzy, particularly in its mantic aspect. It is surprising that Ninck does
not mention Hermes, the god of revelation, who as *pneuma* and

12 *Wodan und germanischer Schicksalsglaube.*
13 [*Wunsch,* magical wish; *Minne,* remembrance, love; *Einherier,* the dead heroes
in Valhalla (*Meyers Konversations-Lexikon*).—EDITORS.]
14 [*Fylgja,* attendant spirit in the form of an animal (Hastings, *Encyclopedia*).]

nous is associated with the wind. He would be the connecting-link with the Christian pneuma and the miracle of Pentecost. As Poimandres (the shepherd of men) Hermes is an *Ergreifer* like Wotan. Ninck rightly points out that Dionysus and the other Greek gods always remained under the supreme authority of Zeus, which indicates a fundamental difference between the Greek and the Germanic temperament. Ninck assumes an inner affinity between Wotan and Kronos, and the latter's defeat may perhaps be a sign that the Wotan-archetype was once overcome and split up in prehistoric times. At all events, the Germanic god represents a totality on a very primitive level, a psychological condition in which man's will was almost identical with the god's and entirely at his mercy. But the Greeks had gods who helped man against other gods; indeed, All-Father Zeus himself is not far from the ideal of a benevolent, enlightened despot.

It was not in Wotan's nature to linger on and show signs of old age. He simply disappeared when the times turned against him, and remained invisible for more than a thousand years, working anonymously and indirectly. Archetypes are like river-beds which dry up when the water deserts them, but which it can find again at any time. An archetype is like an old water-course along which the water of life has flowed for centuries, digging a deep channel for itself. The longer it has flowed in this channel the more likely it is that sooner or later the water will return to its old bed. The life of the individual as a member of society and particularly as part of the State may be regulated like a canal, but the life of nations is a great rushing river which is utterly beyond human control, in the hands of One who has always been stronger than men. The League of Nations, which was supposed to possess supranational authority, is regarded by some as a child in need of care and protection, by others as an abortion. Thus the life of nations rolls on unchecked, without guidance, unconscious of where it is going, like a rock crashing down the side of a hill, until it is stopped by an obstacle stronger than itself. Political events move from one impasse to the next, like a torrent caught in gullies, creeks, and marshes. All human control comes to an end when the individual is caught in a mass movement. Then the archetypes begin to function, as happens also in the lives of individuals when they are confronted with situations that cannot be dealt with in any of the familiar ways.

20

But what a so-called Führer does with a mass movement can plainly be seen if we turn our eyes to the north or south of our country.

The ruling archetype does not remain the same for ever, as is evident from the temporal limitations that have been set to the hoped-for reign of peace, the "thousand-year Reich." The Mediterranean father-archetype of the just, order-loving, benevolent ruler has been shattered over the whole of northern Europe, as the present fate of the Christian Churches bears witness. Fascism in Italy and the civil war in Spain show that in the south as well the cataclysm has been far greater than one expected. Even the Catholic Church can no longer afford trials of strength.

The nationalist God has attacked Christianity on a broad front. In Russia he is called technology and science, in Italy, Duce, and in Germany, "German Faith," "German Christianity," or the State. The "German Christians" [15] are a contradiction in terms and would do better to join Hauer's "German Faith Movement." [16] These are decent and well-meaning people.

[15] A National Socialist movement inside the Protestant Church, which tried to eliminate all vestiges of the Old Testament from Christianity.

[16] Wilhelm Hauer (b. 1881), first a missionary and later professor of Sanskrit at the University of Tübingen, was the founder and leader of the "German Faith Movement." It tried to establish a "German Faith" founded on German and Nordic writings and traditions, e.g., those of Eckhart and Goethe. This movement sought to combine a number of different and often incompatible trends: some of its members accepted an expurgated form of Christianity, others were opposed not only to Christianity in any form but to every kind of religion or god. One of the common articles of faith, which the movement adopted in 1934, was: "The German Faith Movement aims at the religious renaissance of the nation out of the hereditary foundations of the German race."

The spirit of this movement may be contrasted with a sermon preached by Dr. Langmann, an evangelical clergyman and high dignitary of the Church, at the funeral of the late Gustloff. Dr. Langmann gave the address "in S.A. uniform and jackboots." He sped the deceased on his journey to Hades, and directed him to Valhalla, to the home of Siegfried and Baldur, the heroes who "nourish the life of the German people by the sacrifice of their blood"—like Christ among others. "May this god send the nations of the earth *clanking on their way* through history." "Lord bless our struggle. Amen." Thus the reverend gentleman ended his address, according to the *Neue Zürcher Zeitung* (1936, no. 249). As a service held to Wotan it is no doubt very edifying—and remarkably tolerant towards believers in Christ! Are our Churches inclined to be equally tolerant and to preach that Christ shed his blood for the salvation of mankind, like Siegfried, Baldur, and Odin among others?! One can ask unexpectedly grotesque questions these days.

21

who honestly admit their *Ergriffenheit* and try to come to terms with this new and undeniable fact. They go to an enormous amount of trouble to make it look less alarming by dressing it up in a conciliatory historical garb and giving us consoling glimpses of great figures such as Meister Eckhart, who was also a German and also *ergriffen*. In this way the awkward question of who the *Ergreifer* is is circumvented. He was always "God." But the more Hauer restricts the world-wide sphere of Indo-European culture to the "Nordic" in general and to the *Edda* in particular, and the more "German" this faith becomes as a manifestation of *Ergriffenheit*, the more painfully evident it is that the "German" god is the god of the Germans.

One cannot read Hauer's book [17] without emotion, if one regards it as the tragic and really heroic effort of a conscientious scholar who, without knowing how it happened to him, was violently summoned by the inaudible voice of the *Ergreifer* and is now trying with all his might, and with all his knowledge and ability, to build a bridge between the dark forces of life and the shining world of historical ideas. But what do all the beauties of the past from totally different levels of culture mean to the man of today, when confronted with a living and unfathomable tribal god such as he has never experienced before? They are sucked like dry leaves into the roaring whirlwind, and the rhythmic alliterations of the *Edda* become inextricably mixed up with Christian mystical texts, German poetry, and the wisdom of the *Upanishads*. Hauer himself is *ergriffen* by the depths of meaning in the primal words lying at the root of the Germanic languages, to an extent that he certainly never knew before. Hauer the Indologist is not to blame for this, nor yet the *Edda;* it is rather the fault of *kairos*—the present moment in time—whose name on closer investigation turns out to be Wotan. I would therefore advise the German Faith Movement to throw aside their scruples. Intelligent people will not confuse them with the crude Wotan-worshippers whose faith is a mere pretence. There are people in the German Faith Movement who are intelligent enough not only to *believe* but to *know* that the god of the *Germans* is Wotan and not the Christian God. This is a tragic experience and no disgrace. It has always been terrible to fall

17 *Deutsche Gottschau: Grundzüge eines deutschen Glaubens* [German Vision of God: Basic Elements of a German Faith].

into the hands of a living god. Yahweh was no exception to this rule, and the Philistines, Edomites, Amorites, and the rest, who were outside the Yahweh experience, must certainly have found it exceedingly disagreeable. The Semitic [18] experience of Allah was for a long time an extremely painful affair for the whole of Christendom. We who stand outside judge the Germans far too much as if they were responsible agents, but perhaps it would be nearer the truth to regard them also as *victims*.

If we apply our admittedly peculiar point of view consistently, we are driven to conclude that Wotan must, in time, reveal not only the restless, violent, stormy side of his character, but also his ecstatic and mantic qualities—a very different aspect of his nature. If this conclusion is correct, National Socialism would not be the last word. Things must be concealed in the background which we cannot imagine at present, but we may expect them to appear in the course of the next few years or decades. Wotan's reawakening is a stepping back into the past; the stream was dammed up and has broken into its old channel. But the obstruction will not last for ever; it is rather a *reculer pour mieux sauter,* and the water will overleap the obstacle. Then at last we shall know what Wotan is saying when he "murmurs with Mimir's head."

> Fast move the sons   of Mim, and fate
> Is heard in the note   of the Gjallarhorn;
> Loud blows Heimdall,   the horn is aloft,
> In fear quake all   who on Hel-roads are.
>
> Yggdrasil shakes   and shivers on high
> The ancient limbs,   and the giant is loose;
> Wotan murmurs   with Mimir's head
> But the kinsman of Surt   shall slay him soon.
>
> How fare the gods?   how fare the elves?
> All Jotunheim groans,   the gods are at council;
> Loud roar the dwarfs   by the doors of stone,
> The masters of the rocks: would you know yet more?

[18] [Using the word to connote those peoples within the Semitic language-group. —TRANS.]

23

Now Garm howls loud   before Gnipahellir;
The fetters will burst,   and the wolf run free;
Much do I know,   and more can see
Of the fate of the gods,   the mighty in fight.

From the east comes Hrym   with shield held high;
In giant-wrath   does the serpent writhe;
O'er the waves he twists,   and the tawny eagle
Gnaws corpses screaming;   Naglfar is loose.

O'er the sea from the north   there sails a ship
With the people of Hel,   at the helm stands Loki;
After the wolf   do wild men follow,
And with them the brother   of Byleist goes.[19]

[19] *Voluspo* (*The Poetic Edda,* trans. by Bellows, pp. 20f.; line 7 mod.).

3

Psychotherapy Today[1]

It would be a rewarding task to examine in some detail the relationship between psychotherapy and the state of mind in Europe today. Yet probably no one would be blamed for shrinking from so bold a venture, for who could guarantee that the picture he has formed of the present psychological and spiritual plight of Europe is true to reality? Are we, as contemporaries of and participants in these cataclysmic events, at all capable of cool judgment and of seeing clearly amid the indescribable political and ideological chaos of present-day Europe? Or should we perhaps do better to narrow the field of psychotherapy and restrict our science to a modest specialists' corner, remaining indifferent to the ruin of half the world? I fear that such a course, in spite of its commendable modesty, would ill accord with the nature of psychotherapy, which is after all the "treatment of the soul." Indeed, the concept of psychotherapy, however one may choose to interpret it, carries with it very great pretensions: for the soul is the birth-place of all action and hence of everything that happens by the will of man. It would be difficult, if not impossible, to carve out an arbitrarily limited segment of the infinitely vast realm of the psyche and call that the secluded theatre of psychotherapy. Medicine, it is true, has found itself obliged to mark off a specific field, that of the neuroses and psychoses, and this is both convenient and feasible for the practical purpose of treatment. But the artificial restriction must be broken down immediately psychotherapy understands its problems not simply as those of a technique but as

[1] [A lecture delivered to a Section of the Swiss Society for Psychotherapy at its fourth annual meeting (1941). The Section was formed to further the interests of psychotherapists in Switzerland. The lecture was published as "Die Psychotherapie in der Gegenwart" in the *Schweizerische Zeitschrift für Psychologie und ihre Anwendungen*, IV (1945), 1–18.]

those of a science. Science *qua* science has no boundaries, and there is no speciality whatever that can boast of complete self-sufficiency. Any speciality is bound to spill over its borders and to encroach on adjoining territory if it is to lay serious claim to the status of a science. Even so highly specialized a technique as Freudian psychoanalysis was unable, at the very outset, to avoid poaching on other, and sometimes exceedingly remote, scientific preserves. It is, in fact, impossible to treat the psyche, and human personality in general, sectionally. In all psychic disturbances it is becoming clear—perhaps even more so than in the case of physical illnesses—that the psyche is a whole in which everything hangs together. When the patient comes to us with a neurosis, he does not bring a part but the whole of his psyche and with it the fragment of world on which that psyche depends, and without which it can never be properly understood. Psychotherapy is therefore less able than any other specialized department of science to take refuge in the sanctuary of a speciality which has no further connection with the world at large. Try as we may to concentrate on the most personal of personal problems, our therapy nevertheless stands or falls with the question: What sort of world does our patient come from and to what sort of world has he to adapt himself? The world is a supra-personal fact to which an essentially personalistic psychology can never do justice. Such a psychology only penetrates to the personal element in man. But in so far as he is also a part of the world, he carries the world in himself, that is, something at once impersonal and supra-personal. It includes his entire physical and psychic basis, so far as this is given from the start. Undoubtedly the personalities of father and mother form the first and apparently the only world of man as an infant; and, if they continue to do so for too long, he is on the surest road to neurosis, because the great world he will have to enter as a whole person is no longer a world of fathers and mothers, but a supra-personal fact. The child first begins to wean itself from the childhood relation to father and mother through its relation to its brothers and sisters. The elder brother is no longer the true father and the elder sister no longer the true mother. Later, husband and wife are originally strangers to one another and come from different families with a different history and often a different social background. When children

26

come, they complete the process by forcing the parents into the role of father and mother, which the parents, in accordance with their infantile attitude, formerly saw only in others, thereby trying to secure for themselves all the advantages of the childhood role. Every more or less normal life runs this enantiodromian course and compels a change of attitude from the extreme of the child to the other extreme of the parent. The change requires the recognition of objective facts and values which a child can dismiss from his mind. School, however, inexorably instils into him the idea of objective time, of duty and the fulfilment of duty, of outside authority, no matter whether he likes or loathes the school and his teacher. And with school and the relentless advance of time, one objective fact after another increasingly forces its way into his personal life, regardless of whether it is welcome or not and whether he has developed any special attitude towards it. Meanwhile it is made overpoweringly clear that any prolongation of the father-and-mother world beyond its allotted span must be paid for dearly. All attempts to carry the infant's personal world over into the greater world are doomed to failure; even the transference which occurs during the treatment of neurosis is at best only an intermediate stage, giving the patient a chance to shed all the fragments of egg-shell still adhering to him from his childhood days, and to withdraw the projection of the parental imagos from external reality. This operation is one of the most difficult tasks of modern psychotherapy. At one time it was optimistically assumed that the parental imagos could be more or less broken down and destroyed through analysis of their contents. But in reality that is not the case: although the parental imagos can be released from the state of projection and withdrawn from the external world, they continue, like everything else acquired in early childhood, to retain their original freshness. With the withdrawal of the projection they fall back into the individual psyche, from which indeed they mainly originated.[2]

Before we go into the question of what happens when the parental imagos are no longer projected, let us turn to another question: Is this problem, which has been brought to light by

2 As we know, the parental imago is constituted on the one hand by the personally acquired image of the personal parents, but on the other hand by the parent archetype which exists a priori, i.e., in the pre-conscious structure of the psyche.

modern psychotherapy, a new one in the sense that it was unknown to earlier ages which possessed no scientific psychology
as we understand it? How did this problem present itself in the
past?

In so far as earlier ages had in fact no knowledge of psychotherapy in our sense of the word, we cannot possibly expect to
find in history any formulations similar to our own. But since
the transformation of child into parent has been going on
everywhere from time immemorial and, with the increase of
consciousness, was also experienced subjectively as a difficult
process, we must conjecture the existence of various general
psychotherapeutic systems which enabled man to accomplish
the difficult transition-stages. And we do find, even at the most
primitive level, certain drastic measures at all those moments in
life when psychic transitions have to be effected. The most important of these are the initiations at puberty and the rites per-
taining to marriage, birth, and death. All these ceremonies,
which in primitive cultures still free from foreign influence are
observed with the utmost care and exactitude, are probably
designed in the first place to avert the psychic injuries liable to
occur at such times; but they are also intended to impart to the
initiand the preparation and teaching needed for life. The
existence and prosperity of a primitive tribe are absolutely
bound up with the scrupulous and traditional performance of
the ceremonies. Wherever these customs fall into disuse through
the influence of the white man, authentic tribal life ceases; the
tribe loses its soul and disintegrates. Opinion is very much
divided about the influence of Christian missionaries in this
respect; what I myself saw in Africa led me to take an extremely
pessimistic view.

On a higher and more civilized level the same work is performed by the great religions. There are the christening, con-
firmation, marriage, and funeral ceremonies which, as is well
known, are much closer to their origins, more living and complete, in Catholic ritual than in Protestantism. Here too we see
how the father-mother world of the child is superseded by a
wealth of analogical symbols: a patriarchal order receives the
adult into a new filial relationship through spiritual generation
and rebirth. The pope as *pater patrum* and the *ecclesia mater*
are the parents of a family that embraces the whole of Christen-

28

dom, except such parts of it as protest. Had the parental imagos been destroyed in the course of development and thus been rendered ineffective, an order of this kind would have lost not only its *raison d'être* but the very possibility of its existence. As it is, however, a place is found for the ever-active parental imagos as well as for that ineradicable feeling of being a child, a feeling which finds meaning and shelter in the bosom of the Church. In addition, a number of other ecclesiastical institutions provide for the steady growth and constant renewal of the bond. Among them I would mention in particular the mass and the confessional. The Communion is, in the proper sense of the word, the family table at which the members foregather and partake of the meal in the presence of God, following a sacred custom that goes far back into pre-Christian times.

It is superfluous to describe these familiar things in greater detail. I mention them only to show that the treatment of the psyche in times gone by had in view the same fundamental facts of human life as modern psychotherapy. But how differently religion deals with the parental imagos! It does not dream of breaking them down or destroying them; on the contrary, it recognizes them as living realities which it would be neither possible nor profitable to eliminate. Religion lets them live on in changed and exalted form within the framework of a strictly traditional patriarchal order, which keeps not merely decades but whole centuries in living connection. Just as it nurtures and preserves the childhood psyche of the individual, so also it has conserved numerous and still living vestiges of the childhood psyche of humanity. In this way it guards against one of the greatest psychic dangers—loss of roots—which is a disaster not only for primitive tribes but for civilized man as well. The breakdown of a tradition, necessary as this may be at times, is always a loss and a danger; and it is a danger to the soul because the life of instinct—the most conservative element in man—always expresses itself in traditional usages. Age-old convictions and customs are deeply rooted in the instincts. If they get lost, the conscious mind becomes severed from the instincts and loses its roots, while the instincts, unable to express themselves, fall back into the unconscious and reinforce its energy, causing this in turn to overflow into the existing contents of consciousness. It is then that the rootless condition of consciousness becomes a real danger. This secret *vis a tergo* results in a hybris of the conscious mind which manifests itself in the form of exaggerated self-esteem or an inferiority complex. At all events a loss of balance ensues, and this is the most fruitful soil for psychic injury.

If we look back over the thousand-odd years of our European civilization, we shall see that the Western ideal of the education and care of the soul has been, and for the most part still is, a patriarchal order based on the recognition of parental imagos. Thus in dealing with the individual, no matter how revolutionary his conscious attitude may be, we have to reckon with a patriarchal or hierarchical orientation of the psyche which causes it instinctively to seek and cling to this order. Any attempt to render the parental imagos and the childhood psyche ineffective is therefore doomed to failure from the outset.

At this point we come back to our earlier question of what happens when the parental imagos are withdrawn from projection. The detachment of these imagos from certain persons who carry the projection is undoubtedly possible and belongs to the stock in trade of psychotherapeutic success. On the other hand the problem becomes more difficult when there is a transference of the imagos to the doctor. In these cases the detachment can develop into a crucial drama. For what is to happen to the imagos if they are no longer attached to a human being? The pope as supreme father of Christendom holds his office from God; he is the servant of servants, and transference of the imagos to him is thus a transference to the Father in heaven and to Mother Church on earth. But how fares it with men and women who have been uprooted and torn out of their tradition? Professor Murray[3] of Harvard University has shown on the basis of extensive statistical material—thus confirming my own previously published experience—that the incidence of complexes is, on the average, highest among Jews; second come Protestants; and Catholics third. That a man's philosophy of life is directly connected with the well-being of the psyche can be seen from the fact that his mental attitude, his way of looking at things, is of enormous importance to him and his mental health—so much so that we could almost say that things are less what they

[3] In *Explorations in Personality.*

30

are than how we see them. If we have a disagreeable view of a situation or thing, our pleasure in it is spoiled, and then it does in fact usually disagree with us. And, conversely, how many things become bearable and even acceptable if we can give up certain prejudices and change our point of view. Paracelsus, who was above all a physician of genius, emphasized that nobody could be a doctor who did not understand the art of "theorizing." [4] What he meant was that the doctor must induce, not only in himself but also in his patient, a way of looking at the illness which would enable the doctor to cure and the patient to recover, or at least to endure being ill. That is why he says "every illness is a purgatorial fire." [5] He consciously recognized and made full use of the healing power of a man's mental attitude. When, therefore, I am treating practising Catholics, and am faced with the transference problem, I can, by virtue of my office as a doctor, step aside and lead the problem over to the Church. But if I am treating a non-Catholic, that way out is debarred, and by virtue of my office as a doctor I cannot step aside, for there is as a rule nobody there, nothing towards which I could suitably lead the father-imago. I can, of course, get the patient to recognize with his reason that I am not the father. But by that very act I become the reasonable father and remain despite everything the father. Not only nature, but the patient too, abhors a vacuum. He has an instinctive horror of allowing the parental imagos and his childhood psyche to fall into nothingness, into a hopeless past that has no future. His instinct tells him that, for the sake of his own wholeness, these things must be kept alive in one form or another. He knows that a complete withdrawal of the projection will be followed by an apparently endless isolation within the ego, which is all the more burdensome because he has so little love for it. He found it unbearable enough before, and he is unlikely to bear it now simply out of sweet reasonableness. Therefore at this juncture the Catholic who has been freed from an excessively personal tie to his parents can return fairly easily to the mysteries of the Church, which he is now in a position to understand better and more deeply. There are also Protestants

4 * "Labyrinthus medicorum errantium," p. 199 ("Theorica medica"). [The word θεωρία originally meant looking about one at the world.—TRANS.]
5 * "De ente Dei," p. 226.

who can discover in one of the newer variants of Protestantism a meaning which appeals to them, and so regain a genuine religious attitude. All other cases—unless there is a violent and sometimes injurious solution—will, as the saying goes, "get stuck" in the transference relationship, thereby subjecting both themselves and the doctor to a severe trial of patience. Probably this cannot be avoided, for a sudden fall into the orphaned, parentless state may in certain cases—namely, where there is a tendency to psychosis—have dangerous consequences owing to the equally sudden activation of the unconscious which always accompanies it. Accordingly the projection can and should be withdrawn only step by step. The integration of the contents split off in the parental imagos has an activating effect on the unconscious, for these imagos are charged with all the energy they originally possessed in childhood, thanks to which they continued to exercise a fateful influence even on the adult. Their integration therefore means a considerable afflux of energy to the unconscious, which soon makes itself felt in the increasingly strong coloration of the conscious mind by unconscious contents. Isolation in pure ego-consciousness has the paradoxical consequence that there now appear in dreams and fantasies impersonal, collective contents which are the very material from which certain schizophrenic psychoses are constructed. For this reason the situation is not without its dangers, since the releasing of the ego from its ties with the projection—and of these the transference to the doctor plays the principal part—involves the risk that the ego, which was formerly dissolved in relationships to the personal environment, may now be dissolved in the contents of the collective unconscious. For, although the parents may be dead in the world of external reality, they and their imagos have passed over into the "other" world of the collective unconscious, where they continue to attract the same ego-dissolving projections as before.

But at this point a healthful, compensatory operation comes into play which each time seems to me like a miracle. Struggling against that dangerous trend towards disintegration, there arises out of this same collective unconscious a counter-action, characterized by symbols which point unmistakably to a process of centring. This process creates nothing less than

32

a new centre of personality, which the symbols show from the first to be superordinate to the ego and which later proves its superiority empirically. The centre cannot therefore be classed with the ego, but must be accorded a higher value. Nor can we continue to give it the name of "ego," for which reason I have called it the "self." To experience and realize this self is the ultimate aim of Indian yoga, and in considering the psychology of the self we would do well to have recourse to the treasures of Indian wisdom. In India, as with us, the experience of the self has nothing to do with intellectualism; it is a vital happening which brings about a fundamental transformation of personality. I have called the process that leads to this experience the "process of individuation." If I recommend the study of classical yoga, it is not because I am one of those who roll up their eyes in ecstasy when they hear such magic words as *dhyana* or *buddhi* or *mukti,* but because psychologically we can learn a great deal from yoga philosophy and turn it to practical account. Furthermore, the material lies ready to hand, clearly formulated in the Eastern books and the translations made of them. Here again my reason is not that we have nothing equivalent in the West: I recommend yoga merely because the Western knowledge which is akin to it is more or less inaccessible except to specialists. It is esoteric, and it is distorted beyond recognition by being formulated as an arcane discipline and by all the rubbish that this draws in its wake. In alchemy there lies concealed a Western system of yoga meditation, but it was kept a carefully guarded secret from fear of heresy and its painful consequences. For the practising psychologist, however, alchemy has one inestimable advantage over Indian yoga—its ideas are expressed almost entirely in an extraordinarily rich symbolism, the very symbolism we still find in our patients today. The help which alchemy affords us in understanding the symbols of the individuation process is, in my opinion, of the utmost importance.[6]

Alchemy describes what I call the "self" as *incorruptibile,* that is, an indissoluble substance, a One and Indivisible that cannot be reduced to anything else and is at the same time a Universal, to which a sixteenth-century alchemist even gave the

[6] Cf. *Psychology and Alchemy,* and "Psychology and Religion."

name of *filius macrocosmi*.[7] Modern findings agree in principle with these formulations.

I had to mention all these things in order to get to the problem of today. For if we perseveringly and consistently follow the way of natural development, we arrive at the experience of the self, and at the state of being simply what one is. This is expressed as an ethical demand by the motto of Paracelsus, the four-hundredth anniversary of whose birth we celebrated in the autumn of 1941: "Alterius non sit, qui suus esse potest" (That man no other man shall own,/Who to himself belongs alone)—a motto both characteristically Swiss and characteristically alchemical. But the way to this goal is toilsome and not for all to travél. "Est longissima via," say the alchemists. We are still only at the beginning of a development whose origins lie in late antiquity, and which throughout the Middle Ages led little more than a hole-and-corner existence, vegetating in obscurity and represented by solitary eccentrics who were called, not without reason, *tenebriones*. Nevertheless men like Albertus Magnus, Roger Bacon, and Paracelsus were among the fathers of modern science, and their spirit did much to shake the authority of the "total" Church. Our modern psychology grew out of the spirit of natural science and, without realizing it, is carrying on the work begun by the alchemists. These men were convinced that the *donum artis* was given only to the few *electis*, and today our experience shows us only too plainly how arduous is the work with each patient and how few can attain the necessary knowledge and experience. Meanwhile the disintegration and weakening of that salutary institution, the Christian Church, goes on at an alarming rate, and the loss of any firm authority is gradually leading to an intellectual, political, and social anarchy which is repugnant to the soul of European man, accustomed as he is to a patriarchal order. The present attempts to achieve full individual consciousness and to mature the personality are, socially speaking, still so feeble that they carry no weight at all in relation to our historic needs. If our European social order is not to be shaken to its foundations, authority must be restored at all costs.

7 Khunrath, *Von hylealischen . . . Chaos.*

This is probably one reason for the efforts now being made in Europe to replace the collectivity of the Church by the collectivity of the State. And just as the Church was once absolute in its determination to make theocracy a reality, so the State is now making an absolute bid for totalitarianism. The mystique of the spirit has not been replaced by a mystique either of nature or of the *lumen naturae*, as Paracelsus named it, but by the total incorporation of the individual in a political collective called the "State." This offers a way out of the dilemma, for the parental imagos can now be projected upon the State as the universal provider and the authority responsible for all thinking and willing. The ends of science are made to serve the social collective and are only valued for their practical utility to the collective's ends. The natural course of psychological development is succeeded, not by a spiritual direction which spans the centuries and keeps cultural values alive, but by a political directorate which ministers to the power struggles of special groups and promises economic benefits to the masses. In this way European man's deep-seated longing for a patriarchal and hierarchical order finds an appropriate concrete expression which accords only too well with the herd instinct, but is fixed at such a low level as to be in every respect detrimental to culture.

It is here that opinion is apt to be divided. In so far as psychotherapy claims to stand on a scientific basis and thus by the principle of free investigation, its declared aim is to educate people towards independence and moral freedom in accordance with the knowledge arrived at by unprejudiced scientific research. Whatever the conditions to which the individual wishes to adapt himself, he should always do so consciously and of his own free choice. But, in so far as political aims and the State are to claim precedence, psychotherapy would inevitably become the instrument of a particular political system, and it is to *its* aims that people would have to be educated and at the same time seduced from their own highest destiny. Against this conclusion it will undoubtedly be objected that man's ultimate destiny lies not in his existence as an individual but in the aspirations of human society, because without this the individual could not exist at all. This objection is a weighty one and cannot be lightly dismissed. It is an undoubted truth that the individual exists only by virtue of society and has always so existed. That is why among primitive tribes we find the custom of initiation into manhood, when, by means of a ritual death, the individual is detached from his family and indeed from his whole previous identity, and is reborn as a member of the tribe. Or we find early civilizations, such as the Egyptian and Babylonian, where all individuality is concentrated in the person of the king, while the ordinary person remains anonymous. Or again, we observe whole families in which for generations the individuality of the name has compensated for the nonentity of its bearers; or a long succession of Japanese artists who discard their own name and adopt the name of a master, simply adding after it a modest numeral. Nevertheless, it was the great and imperishable achievement of Christianity that, in contrast to these archaic systems which are all based on the original projection of psychic contents, it gave to each individual man the dignity of an immortal soul, whereas in earlier times this prerogative was reserved to the sole person of the king. It would lead me too far to discuss here just how much this Christian innovation represents an advance of human consciousness and of culture in general, by putting an end to the projection of the highest values of the individual soul upon the king or other dignitaries. The innate will to consciousness, to moral freedom and culture, proved stronger than the brute compulsion of projections which keep the individual permanently imprisoned in the dark of unconsciousness and grind him down into nonentity. Certainly this advance laid a cross upon him—the torment of consciousness, of moral conflict, and the uncertainty of his own thoughts. This task is so immeasurably difficult that it can be accomplished, if at all, only by stages, century by century, and it must be paid for by endless suffering and toil in the struggle against all those powers which are incessantly at work persuading us to take the apparently easier road of unconsciousness. Those who go the way of unconsciousness imagine that the task can safely be left to "others" or, ultimately, to the anonymous State. But who are these "others," these obvious supermen who pretend to be able to do what everybody is only too ready to believe that he cannot do? They are men just like ourselves, who think and feel as we do, except that they are past masters in the art of "passing the buck." Exactly *who* is the State?—The agglomeration of all the nonentities composing it. Could it be personified, the result would be an individual, or rather a monster, intellectually and ethically far below the level of most of the individuals in it, since it represents mass psychology raised to the *n*th power. Therefore Christianity in its best days never subscribed to a belief in the State, but set before man a supramundane goal which should redeem him from the compulsive force of his projections upon this world, whose ruler is the spirit of darkness. And it gave him an immortal soul that he might have a fulcrum from which to lift the world off its hinges, showing him that his goal lies not in the mastery of this world but in the attainment of the Kingdom of God, whose foundations are in his own heart.

If, then, man cannot exist without society, neither can he exist without oxygen, water, albumen, fat, and so forth. Like these, society is one of the necessary conditions of his existence. It would be ludicrous to maintain that man lives in order to breathe air. It is equally ludicrous to say that the individual exists for society. "Society" is nothing more than a term, a concept for the symbiosis of a group of human beings. A concept is not a carrier of life. The sole and natural carrier of life is the individual, and that is so throughout nature.[8] "Society" or "State" is an agglomeration of life-carriers and at the same time, as an organized form of these, an important condition of life. It is therefore not quite true to say that the individual can exist only as a particle in society. At all events man can live very much longer without the State than without air.

---

[8] Pestalozzi said (*Ideen*, p. 187): "None of the institutions, measures, and means of education established for the masses and the needs of men in the aggregate, whatever shape or form they may take, serve to advance human culture. In the vast majority of cases they are completely worthless for that purpose and are directly opposed to it. Our race develops its human qualities in essence only from face to face, from heart to heart. Essentially it develops only in little intimate circles which gradually grow in graciousness and love, in confidence and trust. All the means requisite for the education of man, which serve to make him truly humane and to bring him to mankindliness, are in their origin and essence the concern of the individual and of such institutions as are closely and intimately attached to his heart and mind. They never were nor will be the concern of the masses. They never were nor will be the concern of civilization." [See note 10 below.—TRANS.]

When the political aim predominates there can be no doubt that a secondary thing has been made the primary thing. Then the individual is cheated of his rightful destiny and two thousand years of Christian civilization are wiped out. Consciousness, instead of being widened by the withdrawal of projections, is narrowed, because society, a mere condition of human existence, is set up as a goal. Society is the greatest temptation to unconsciousness, for the mass infallibly swallows up the individual—who has no security in himself—and reduces him to a helpless particle. The totalitarian State could not tolerate for one moment the right of psychotherapy to help man fulfil his natural destiny. On the contrary, it would be bound to insist that psychotherapy should be nothing but a tool for the production of manpower useful to the State. In this way it would become a mere technique tied to a single aim, that of increasing social efficiency. The soul would forfeit all life of its own and become a function to be used as the State saw fit. The science of psychology would be degraded to a study of the ways and means to exploit the psychic apparatus. As to its therapeutic aim, the complete and successful incorporation of the patient into the State machine would be the criterion of cure. Since this aim can best be achieved by making the individual completely soulless—that is, as unconscious as possible—all methods designed to increase consciousness would at one stroke become obsolete, and the best thing would be to bring out of the lumber-rooms of the past all the methods that have ever been devised to prevent man from becoming conscious of his unconscious contents. Thus the art of psychotherapy would be driven into a complete regression.[9]

9 Ibid., pp. 189f.: "The collective existence of our race can only produce civilization, not culture. [See note 10 below.—TRANS.] Is it not true, do we not see every day, that in proportion as the herd-like aggregations of men become more important, and in proportion as officialdom, which represents the legal concentration of the power of the masses, has freer play and wields greater authority, the divine breath of tenderness is the more easily extinguished in the hearts of the individuals composing these human aggregations and their officials, and that the receptivity to truth which lies deep in man's nature perishes within them to the same degree?

"The collectively unified man, if truly he be nothing but that, sinks down in all his relations into the depths of civilized corruption, and sunk in this corruption, ceases to seek more over the whole earth than the wild animals in the forest seek."

Such, in broad outline, is the alternative facing psychotherapy at this present juncture. Future developments will decide whether Europe, which fancied it had escaped the Middle Ages, is to be plunged for a second time and for centuries into the darkness of an Inquisition. This will only happen if the totalitarian claims of the State are forcibly carried through and become a permanency. No intelligent person will deny that the organization of society, which we call the State, not only feels a lively need to extend its authority but is compelled by circumstances to do so. If this comes about by free consent and the conscious choice of the public, the results will leave nothing to be desired. But if it comes about for the sake of convenience, in order to avoid tiresome decisions, or from lack of consciousness, then the individual runs the certain risk of being blotted out as a responsible human being. The State will then be no different from a prison or an ant-heap.

Although the conscious achievement of individuality is consistent with man's natural destiny, it is nevertheless not his whole aim. It cannot possibly be the object of human education to create an anarchic conglomeration of individual existences. That would be too much like the unavowed ideal of extreme individualism, which is essentially no more than a morbid reaction against an equally futile collectivism. In contrast to all this, the natural process of individuation brings to birth a consciousness of human community precisely because it makes us aware of the unconscious, which unites and is common to all mankind. Individuation is an at-one-ment with oneself and at the same time with humanity, since oneself is a part of humanity. Once the individual is thus secured in himself, there is some guarantee that the organized accumulation of individuals in the State—even in one wielding greater authority—will result in the formation no longer of an anonymous mass but of a conscious community. The indispensable condition for this is conscious freedom of choice and individual decision. Without this freedom and self-determination there is no true community, and, it must be said, without such community even the free and self-secured individual cannot in the long run prosper.[10]

10 More than a hundred years ago, in times not so unlike our own, Pestalozzi wrote (ibid., p. 186): "The race of men cannot remain socially united without some ordering power. Culture has the power to unite men as individuals, in independence and

Moreover, the common weal is best served by independent personalities. Whether man today possesses the maturity needed for such a decision is another question. On the other hand, solutions which violently forestall natural development and are forced on mankind are equally questionable. The facts of nature cannot in the long run be violated. Penetrating and seeping through everything like water, they will undermine any system that fails to take account of them, and sooner or later they will bring about its downfall. But an authority wise enough in its statesmanship to give sufficient free play to nature—of which spirit is a part—need fear no premature decline. It is perhaps a humiliating sign of spiritual immaturity that European man needs, and wants, a large measure of authority. The fact has to be faced that countless millions in Europe—with the guilty complicity of reformers whose childishness is only equalled by their lack of tradition—have escaped from the authority of the Church and the *patria potestas* of kings and emperors only to fall helpless and senseless victims to any power that cares to assume authority. The immaturity of man is a fact that must enter into all our calculations.

We in Switzerland are not living on a little planetoid revolving in empty space, but on the same earth as the rest of Europe. We are right in the middle of these problems, and if we are unconscious, we are just as likely to succumb to them as the other nations. The most dangerous thing would be for us to imagine that we are on a higher plane of consciousness than our neighbours. There is no question of that. While it would be an impropriety for a handful of psychologists and psychotherapists like ourselves to take our importance too seriously—or I might say, too pompously—I would nevertheless emphasize that just because we are psychologists it is our first task and duty to understand the psychic situation of our time and to see clearly the problems and challenges with which it faces us. Even if our voice

freedom, through law and art. But a cultureless civilization unites them as masses, without regard to independence, freedom, law or art, through the power of coercion." [N.B. Pestalozzi evidently subscribes to the Germanic distinction between *Kultur* and *Zivilisation*, where the latter term is employed in a pejorative sense. The idea is that culture, deriving ultimately from tillage and worship (*cultus*), is a natural organic growth, whereas civilization is an affair of the city (*civis*) and thus something artificial. Cf. note 9 above.—TRANS.]

is too weak to make itself heard above the tumult of political strife and fades away ineffectively, we may yet comfort ourselves with the saying of the Chinese Master: "When the enlightened man is alone and thinks rightly, it can be heard a thousand miles away."

All beginnings are small. Therefore we must not mind doing tedious but conscientious work on obscure individuals, even though the goal towards which we strive seems unattainably far off. But one goal we can attain, and that is to develop and bring to maturity individual personalities. And inasmuch as we are convinced that the individual is the carrier of life, we have served life's purpose if one tree at least succeeds in bearing fruit, though a thousand others remain barren. Anyone who proposed to bring all growing things to the highest pitch of luxuriance would soon find the weeds—those hardiest of perennials—waving above his head. I therefore consider it the prime task of psychotherapy today to pursue with singleness of purpose the goal of individual development. So doing, our efforts will follow nature's own striving to bring life to the fullest possible fruition in each individual, for only in the individual can life fulfil its meaning—not in the bird that sits in a gilded cage.

4

Psychotherapy and
a Philosophy of Life[1]

So much is psychotherapy the child of practical improvisation that for a long time it had trouble in thinking out its own intellectual foundations. Empirical psychology relied very much at first on physical and then on physiological ideas, and ventured only with some hesitation on the complex phenomena which constitute its proper field. Similarly, psychotherapy was at first simply an auxiliary method; only gradually did it free itself from the world of ideas represented by medical therapeutics and come to understand that its concern lay not merely with physiological but primarily with psychological principles. In other words, it found itself obliged to raise psychological issues which soon burst the framework of the experimental psychology of that day with its elementary statements. The demands of therapy brought highly complex factors within the purview of this still young science, and its exponents very often lacked the equipment needed to deal with the problems that arose. It is therefore not surprising that a bewildering assortment of ideas, theories, and points of view predominated in all the initial discussions of this new psychology which had been, so to speak, forced into existence by therapeutic experience. An outsider could hardly be blamed if he received an impression of babel. This confusion was inevitable, for sooner or later it was bound to become clear that one cannot treat the psyche without touching on man and life as a whole, including the ultimate and deepest issues, any more than one can treat the sick body without regard to the totality of its functions—or rather, as a few representatives of modern medicine maintain, the totality of the sick man himself.

[1] [*The introductory address to a discussion at the Conference for Psychology, Zurich, September 26, 1942. Published as "Psychotherapie und Weltanschauung" in the *Schweizerische Zeitschrift für Psychologie und ihre Anwendungen*, I (1943):3, 157–64.]

The more "psychological" a condition is, the greater its complexity and the more it relates to the whole of life. It is true that elementary psychic phenomena are closely allied to physiological processes, and there is not the slightest doubt that the physiological factor forms at least one pole of the psychic cosmos. The instinctive and affective processes, together with all the neurotic symptomatology that arises when these are disturbed, clearly rest on a physiological basis. But, on the other hand, the disturbing factor proves equally clearly that it has the power to turn physiological order into disorder. If the disturbance lies in a repression, then the disturbing factor—that is, the repressive force—belongs to a "higher" psychic order. It is not something elementary and physiologically conditioned, but, as experience shows, a highly complex determinant, as for example certain rational, ethical, aesthetic, religious, or other traditional ideas which cannot be scientifically proved to have any physiological basis. These extremely complex dominants form the other pole of the psyche. Experience likewise shows that this pole possesses an energy many times greater than that of the physiologically conditioned psyche.

With its earliest advances into the field of psychology proper, the new psychotherapy came up against the problem of opposites—a problem that is profoundly characteristic of the psyche. Indeed, the structure of the psyche is so contradictory or contrapuntal that one can scarcely make any psychological assertion or general statement without having immediately to state its opposite.

The problem of opposites offers an eminently suitable and ideal battleground for the most contradictory theories, and above all for partially or wholly unrealized prejudices regarding one's philosophy of life. With this development psychotherapy stirred up a hornets' nest of the first magnitude. Let us take as an example the supposedly simple case of a repressed instinct. If the repression is lifted, the instinct is set free. Once freed, it wants to live and function in its own way. But this creates a difficult—sometimes intolerably difficult—situation. The instinct ought therefore to be modified, or "sublimated," as they say. How this is to be done without creating a new repression nobody can quite explain. The little word "ought" always proves the helplessness of the therapist; it is an admis-

43

sion that he has come to the end of his resources. The final appeal to reason would be very fine if man were by nature a rational animal, but he is not; on the contrary, he is quite as much irrational. Hence reason is often not sufficient to modify the instinct and make it conform to the rational order. Nobody can conceive the moral, ethical, philosophical, and religious conflicts that crop up at this stage of the problem—the facts surpass all imagination. Every conscientious and truth-loving psychotherapist could tell a tale here, though naturally not in public. All the contemporary problems, all the philosophical and religious questionings of our day, are raked up, and unless either the psychotherapist or the patient abandons the attempt in time it is likely to get under both their skins. Each will be driven to a discussion of his philosophy of life, both with himself and with his partner. There are of course forced answers and solutions, but in principle and in the long run they are neither desirable nor satisfying. No Gordian knot can be permanently cut; it has the awkward property of always tying itself again.

This philosophical discussion is a task which psychotherapy necessarily sets itself, though not every patient will come down to basic principles. The question of the measuring rod with which to measure, of the ethical criteria which are to determine our actions, must be answered somehow, for the patient may quite possibly expect us to account for our judgments and decisions. Not all patients allow themselves to be condemned to infantile inferiority because of our refusal to render such an account, quite apart from the fact that a therapeutic blunder of this kind would be sawing off the branch on which we sit. In other words, the art of psychotherapy requires that the therapist be in possession of avowable, credible, and defensible convictions which have proved their viability either by having resolved any neurotic dissociations of his own or by preventing them from arising. A therapist with a neurosis is a contradiction in terms. One cannot help any patient to advance further than one has advanced oneself. On the other hand, the possession of complexes does not in itself signify neurosis, for complexes are the normal foci of psychic happenings, and the fact that they are painful is no proof of pathological disturbance. Suffering is not an illness; it is the normal counterpole to happiness. A complex becomes pathological only when we think we have not got it.

As the most complex of psychic structures, a man's philosophy of life forms the counterpole to the physiologically conditioned psyche, and, as the highest psychic dominant, it ultimately determines the latter's fate. It guides the life of the therapist and shapes the spirit of his therapy. Since it is an essentially subjective system despite the most rigorous objectivity, it may and very likely will be shattered time after time on colliding with the truth of the patient, but it rises again, rejuvenated by the experience. Conviction easily turns into self-defence and is seduced into rigidity, and this is inimical to life. The test of a firm conviction is its elasticity and flexibility; like every other exalted truth it thrives best on the admission of its errors.

I can hardly draw a veil over the fact that we psychotherapists ought really to be philosophers or philosophic doctors—or rather that we already are so, though we are unwilling to admit it because of the glaring contrast between our work and what passes for philosophy in the universities. We could also call it religion *in statu nascendi,* for in the vast confusion that reigns at the roots of life there is no line of division between philosophy and religion. Nor does the unrelieved strain of the psychotherapeutic situation, with its host of impressions and emotional disturbances, leave us much leisure for the systematization of thought. Thus we have no clear exposition of guiding principles drawn from life to offer either to the philosophers or to the theologians.

Our patients suffer from bondage to a neurosis, they are prisoners of the unconscious, and if we attempt to penetrate with understanding into that realm of unconscious forces, we have to defend ourselves against the same influences to which our patients have succumbed. Like doctors who treat epidemic diseases, we expose ourselves to powers that threaten our conscious equilibrium, and we have to take every possible precaution if we want to rescue not only our own humanity but that of the patient from the clutches of the unconscious. Wise self-limitation is not the same thing as text-book philosophy, nor is an ejaculatory prayer in a moment of mortal danger a theological treatise. Both are the outcome of a religious and philosophical attitude that is appropriate to the stark dynamism of life.

The highest dominant always has a religious or a philosophical character. It is by nature extremely primitive, and consequently we find it in full development among primitive peoples. Any difficulty, danger, or critical phase of life immediately calls forth this dominant. It is the most natural reaction to all highly charged emotional situations. But often it remains as obscure as the semiconscious emotional situation which evoked it. Hence it is quite natural that the emotional disturbances of the patient should activate the corresponding religious or philosophical factors in the therapist. Often he is most reluctant to make himself conscious of these primitive contents, and he quite understandably prefers to turn for help to a religion or philosophy which has reached his consciousness from outside. This course does not strike me as being illegitimate in so far as it gives the patient a chance to take his place within the structure of some protective institution existing in the outside world. Such a solution is entirely natural, since there have always and everywhere been totem clans, cults, and creeds whose purpose it is to give an ordered form to the chaotic world of the instincts.

The situation becomes difficult, however, when the patient's nature resists a collective solution. The question then arises whether the therapist is prepared to risk having his convictions dashed and shattered against the truth of the patient. If he wants to go on treating the patient he must abandon all preconceived notions and, for better or worse, go with him in search of the religious and philosophical ideas that best correspond to the patient's emotional states. These ideas present themselves in archetypal form, freshly sprung from the maternal soil whence all religious and philosophical systems originally came. But if the therapist is not prepared to have his convictions called in question for the sake of the patient, then there is some reason for doubting the stability of his basic attitude. Perhaps he cannot give way on grounds of self-defence, which threatens him with rigidity. The margin of psychological elasticity varies both individually and collectively, and often it is so narrow that a certain degree of rigidity really does represent the maximum achievement. *Ultra posse nemo obligatur.*

Instinct is not an isolated thing, nor can it be isolated in practice. It always brings in its train archetypal contents of a spiritual nature, which are at once its foundation and its limitation. In other words, an instinct is always and inevitably coupled with something like a philosophy of life, however archaic, unclear, and hazy this may be. Instinct stimulates thought, and if a man does not think of his own free will, then you get compulsive thinking, for the two poles of the psyche, the physiological and the mental, are indissolubly connected. For this reason instinct cannot be freed without freeing the mind, just as mind divorced from instinct is condemned to futility. Not that the tie between mind and instinct is necessarily a harmonious one. On the contrary it is full of conflict and means suffering. Therefore the principal aim of psychotherapy is not to transport the patient to an impossible state of happiness, but to help him acquire steadfastness and philosophic patience in face of suffering. Life demands for its completion and fulfilment a balance between joy and sorrow. But because suffering is positively disagreeable, people naturally prefer not to ponder how much fear and sorrow fall to the lot of man. So they speak soothingly about progress and the greatest possible happiness, forgetting that happiness is itself poisoned if the measure of suffering has not been fulfilled. Behind a neurosis there is so often concealed all the natural and necessary suffering the patient has been unwilling to bear. We can see this most clearly from hysterical pains, which are relieved in the course of treatment by the corresponding psychic suffering which the patient sought to avoid.

The Christian doctrine of original sin on the one hand, and of the meaning and value of suffering on the other, is therefore of profound therapeutic significance and is undoubtedly far better suited to Western man than Islamic fatalism. Similarly the belief in immortality gives life that untroubled flow into the future so necessary if stoppages and regressions are to be avoided. Although we like to use the word "doctrine" for these —psychologically speaking—extremely important ideas, it would be a great mistake to think that they are just arbitrary intellectual theories. Psychologically regarded, they are emotional experiences whose nature cannot be discussed. If I may permit myself a banal comparison, when I feel well and content no-

47

body can prove to me that I am not. Logical arguments simply bounce off the facts felt and experienced. Original sin, the meaning of suffering, and immortality are emotional facts of this kind. But to experience them is a charisma which no human art can compel. Only unreserved surrender can hope to reach such a goal.

Not everybody is capable of this surrender. There is no "ought" or "must" about it, for the very act of exerting the will inevitably places such an emphasis on *my* will to surrender that the exact opposite of surrender results. The Titans could not take Olympus by storm, and still less may a Christian take Heaven. The most healing, and psychologically the most necessary, experiences are a "treasure hard to attain," and its acquisition demands something out of the common from the common man.

As we know, this something out of the common proves, in practical work with the patient, to be an invasion by archetypal contents. If these contents are to be assimilated, it is not enough to make use of the current philosophical or religious ideas, for they simply do not fit the archaic symbolism of the material. We are therefore forced to go back to pre-Christian and non-Christian conceptions and to conclude that Western man does not possess the monopoly of human wisdom and that the white race is not a species of *Homo sapiens* specially favoured by God. Moreover we cannot do justice to certain contemporary collective phenomena unless we revert to the pre-Christian parallels.

Medieval physicians seem to have realized this, for they practised a philosophy whose roots can be traced back to pre-Christian times and whose nature exactly corresponds to our experiences with patients today. These physicians recognized, besides the light of divine revelation, a *lumen naturae* as a second, independent source of illumination, to which the doctor could turn if the truth as handed down by the Church should for any reason prove ineffective either for himself or for the patient.

It was eminently practical reasons, and not the mere caperings of a hobby-horse, that prompted me to undertake my historical researches. Neither our modern medical training nor academic psychology and philosophy can equip the doctor with

48

the necessary education, or with the means, to deal effectively and understandingly with the often very urgent demands of his psychotherapeutic practice. It therefore behoves us, unembarrassed by our shortcomings as amateurs of history, to go to school once more with the medical philosophers of a distant past, when body and soul had not yet been wrenched asunder into different faculties. Although we are specialists par excellence, our specialized field, oddly enough, drives us to universalism and to the complete overcoming of the specialist attitude, if the totality of body and soul is not to be just a matter of words. Once we have made up our minds to treat the soul, we can no longer close our eyes to the fact that neurosis is not a thing apart but the whole of the pathologically disturbed psyche. It was Freud's momentous discovery that the neurosis is not a mere agglomeration of symptoms, but a wrong functioning which affects the whole psyche. The important thing is not the neurosis, but the man who has the neurosis. We have to set to work on the human being, and we must be able to do him justice as a human being.

The conference we are holding today proves that our psychotherapy has recognized its aim, which is to pay equal attention to the physiological and to the spiritual factor. Originating in natural science, it applies the objective, empirical methods of the latter to the phenomenology of the mind. Even if this should remain a mere attempt, the fact that the attempt has been made is of incalculable significance.

5

After the Catastrophe[1]

This is the first time since 1936 that the fate of Germany again drives me to take up my pen. The quotation from the *Voluspo* with which I ended the article [2] I wrote at that time, about Wotan "murmuring with Mimir's head," pointed prophetically to the nature of the coming apocalyptic events. The myth has been fulfilled, and the greater part of Europe lies in ruins.

Before the work of reconstruction can begin, there is a good deal of clearing up to be done, and this calls above all for *reflection*. Questions are being asked on all sides about the meaning of the whole tragedy. People have even turned to me for an explanation, and I have had to answer them there and then to the best of my ability. But as the spoken word very quickly gives rise to legends, I have decided—not without considerable hesitations and misgivings—to set down my views once again in the form of an article. I am only too well aware that "Germany" presents an immense problem, and that the subjective views of a medical psychologist can touch on only a few aspects of this gigantic tangle of questions. I must be content with a modest contribution to the work of clearing up, without even attempting to look as far ahead as reconstruction.

While I was working on this article I noticed how churned up one still is in one's own psyche, and how difficult it is to reach anything approaching a moderate and relatively calm point of view in the midst of one's emotions. No doubt we should be cold-blooded and superior; but we are, on the whole,

[1] [First published as "Nach der Katastrophe," *Neue Schweizer Rundschau* (Zurich), n.s., XIII (1945), 67–88.]
[2] [See paper on "Wotan," Chapter 2, pp. 10–24.]

much more deeply involved in the recent events in Germany than we like to admit. Nor can we feel compassion, for the heart harbours feelings of a very different nature, and these would like to have the first say. Neither the doctor nor the psychologist can afford to be *only* cold-blooded—quite apart from the fact that they would find it impossible. Their relationship to the world involves them and all their affects, otherwise their relationship would be incomplete. That being so, I found myself faced with the task of steering my ship between Scylla and Charybdis, and —as is usual on such a voyage—stopping my ears to one side of my being and lashing the other to the mast. I must confess that no article has ever given me so much trouble, from a moral as well as a human point of view. I had not realized how much I myself was affected. There are others, I am sure, who will share this feeling with me. This inner identity or *participation mystique* with events in Germany has caused me to experience afresh how painfully wide is the scope of the psychological concept of *collective guilt*. So when I approach this problem it is certainly not with any feelings of cold-blooded superiority, but rather with an avowed sense of inferiority.

The psychological use of the word "guilt" should not be confused with guilt in the legal or moral sense. Psychologically, it connotes the irrational presence of a subjective feeling (or conviction) of guilt, or an objective imputation of, or imputed share in, guilt. As an example of the latter, suppose a man belongs to a family which has the misfortune to be disgraced because one of its members has committed a crime. It is clear that he cannot be held responsible, either legally or morally. Yet the atmosphere of guilt makes itself felt in many ways. His family name appears to have been sullied, and it gives him a painful shock to hear it bandied about in the mouths of strangers. Guilt can be restricted to the lawbreaker only from the legal, moral, and intellectual point of view, but as a psychic phenomenon it spreads itself over the whole neighbourhood. A house, a family, even a village where a murder has been committed feels the psychological guilt and is made to feel it by the outside world. Would one take a room where one knows a man was murdered a few days before? Is it particularly pleasant to marry the sister or daughter of a criminal? What father is not deeply wounded if his son is sent to prison, and does he not feel injured in his

51

family pride if a cousin of the same name brings dishonour on his house? Would not every decent Swiss feel ashamed—to put it mildly—if our Government had erected a human slaughterhouse like Maidenek in our country? Would we then be surprised if, travelling abroad with our Swiss passports, we heard such remarks at the frontier as "Ces cochons de Suisses!"? Indeed, are we not all a little ashamed—precisely because we are patriots—that Switzerland should have bred so many traitors?

Living as we do in the middle of Europe, we Swiss feel comfortably far removed from the foul vapours that arise from the morass of German guilt. But all this changes the moment we set foot, as Europeans, on another continent or come into contact with an Oriental people. What are we to say to an Indian who asks us: "You are anxious to bring us your Christian culture, are you not? May I ask if Auschwitz and Buchenwald are examples of European civilization?" Would it help matters if we hastened to assure him that these things did not take place where we live, but several hundred miles further east—not in our country at all but in a neighbouring one? How would we react if an Indian pointed out indignantly that India's black spot lay not in Travancore but in Hyderabad? Undoubtedly we'd say, "Oh well, India is India!" Similarly, the view all over the East is, "Oh well, Europe is Europe!" The moment we so-called innocent Europeans cross the frontiers of our own continent we are made to feel something of the collective guilt that weighs upon it, despite our good conscience. (One might also ask: Is Russia so primitive that she can still feel our "guilt-by-contagion"— as collective guilt might also be called—and for that reason accuses us of Fascism?) The world sees Europe as the continent on whose soil the shameful concentration camps grew, just as Europe singles out Germany as the land and the people that are enveloped in a cloud of guilt; for the horror happened in Germany and its perpetrators were Germans. No German can deny this, any more than a European or a Christian can deny that the most monstrous crime of all ages was committed in his house. The Christian Church should put ashes on her head and rend her garments on account of the guilt of her children. The shadow of their guilt has fallen on her as much as upon Europe, the mother of monsters. Europe must account for herself before the world, just as Germany must before Europe. The European can no more convince the Indian that Germany is no concern of his, or that he knows nothing at all about that country, than the German can rid himself of his collective guilt by protesting that he did not know. In that way he merely compounds his collective guilt by the sin of unconsciousness.

Psychological collective guilt is a *tragic fate*. It hits everybody, just and unjust alike, everybody who was anywhere near the place where the terrible thing happened. Naturally no reasonable and conscientious person will lightly turn collective into individual guilt by holding the individual responsible without giving him a hearing. He will know enough to distinguish between the individually guilty and the merely collectively guilty. But how many people are either reasonable or conscientious, and how many take the trouble to become so? I am not very optimistic in this respect. Therefore, although collective guilt, viewed on the archaic and primitive level, is a state of *magical uncleanness,* yet precisely because of the general unreasonableness it is a very real fact, which no European outside Europe and no German outside Germany can leave out of account. If the German intends to live on good terms with Europe, he must be conscious that in the eyes of Europeans he is a guilty man. As a German, he has betrayed European civilization and all its values; he has brought shame and disgrace on his European family, so that one must blush to hear oneself called a European; he has fallen on his European brethren like a beast of prey, and tortured and murdered them. The German can hardly expect other Europeans to resort to such niceties as to inquire at every step whether the criminal's name was Müller or Meier. Neither will he be deemed worthy of being treated as a gentleman until the contrary has been proved. Unfortunately, for twelve long years it has been demonstrated with the utmost clarity that the official German was no gentleman.

If a German is prepared to acknowledge his moral inferiority as collective guilt before the whole world, without attempting to minimize it or explain it away with flimsy arguments, then he will stand a reasonable chance, after a time, of being taken for a more or less decent man, and will thus be absolved of his collective guilt at any rate in the eyes of individuals.

It may be objected that the whole concept of psychological collective guilt is a prejudice and a sweepingly unfair condemna-

53

tion. Of course it is, but that is precisely what constitutes the irrational nature of collective guilt: it cares nothing for the just and the unjust, it is the dark cloud that rises up from the scene of an unexpiated crime. It is a psychic phenomenon, and it is therefore no condemnation of the German people to say that they are collectively guilty, but simply a statement of fact. Yet if we penetrate more deeply into the psychology of this phenomenon, we shall soon discover that the problem of collective guilt has another and more questionable aspect than that merely of a collective judgment.

Since no man lives within his own psychic sphere like a snail in its shell, separated from everybody else, but is connected with his fellow-men by his unconscious humanity, no crime can ever be what it appears to our consciousness to be: an isolated psychic happening. In reality, it always happens over a wide radius. The sensation aroused by a crime, the passionate interest in tracking down the criminal, the eagerness with which the court proceedings are followed, and so on, all go to prove the exciting effect which the crime has on everybody who is not abnormally dull or apathetic. Everybody joins in, feels the crime in his own being, tries to understand and explain it. Something is set aflame by that great fire of evil that flared up in the crime. Was not Plato aware that the sight of ugliness produces something ugly in the soul? Indignation leaps up, angry cries of "Justice!" pursue the murderer, and they are louder, more impassioned, and more charged with hate the more fiercely burns the fire of evil that has been lit in our souls. It is a fact that cannot be denied: the wickedness of others becomes our own wickedness because it kindles something evil in our own hearts. The murder has been suffered by everyone, and everyone has committed it; lured by the irresistible fascination of evil, we have all made this collective psychic murder possible; and the closer we were to it and the better we could see, the greater our guilt. In this way we are unavoidably drawn into the uncleanness of evil, no matter what our conscious attitude may be. No one can escape this, for we are all so much a part of the human community that every crime calls forth a secret satisfaction in some corner of the fickle human heart. It is true that, in persons with a strong moral disposition, this reaction may arouse contrary feelings in a neighbouring compartment of the

54

mind. But a strong moral disposition is a comparative rarity, so that when the crimes mount up, indignation may easily get pitched too high, and evil then becomes the order of the day. Everyone harbours his "statistical criminal" in himself, just as he has his own private madman or saint. Owing to this basic peculiarity in our human make-up, a corresponding suggestibility, or susceptibility to infection, exists everywhere. It is our age in particular—the last half century—that has prepared the way for crime. Has it never occurred to anybody, for instance, that the vogue for the thriller has a rather questionable side?

Long before 1933 there was a smell of burning in the air, and people were passionately interested in discovering the locus of the fire and in tracking down the incendiary. And when denser clouds of smoke were seen to gather over Germany, and the burning of the Reichstag gave the signal, then at last there was no mistake where the incendiary, evil in person, dwelt. Terrifying as this discovery was, in time it brought a sense of relief: now we knew for certain where all unrighteousness was to be found, whereas we ourselves were securely entrenched in the opposite camp, among respectable people whose moral indignation could be trusted to rise higher and higher with every fresh sign of guilt on the other side. Even the call for mass executions no longer offended the ears of the righteous, and the saturation bombing of German cities was looked upon as the judgment of God. Hate had found respectable motives and had ceased to be a personal idiosyncrasy, indulged in secret. And all the time the esteemed public had not the faintest idea how closely they themselves were living to evil.

One should not imagine for a moment that anybody could escape this play of opposites. Even a saint would have to pray unceasingly for the souls of Hitler and Himmler, the Gestapo and the S.S., in order to repair without delay the damage done to his own soul. The sight of evil kindles evil in the soul—there is no getting away from this fact. The victim is not the only sufferer; everybody in the vicinity of the crime, including the murderer, suffers with him. Something of the abysmal darkness of the world has broken in on us, poisoning the very air we breathe and befouling the pure water with the stale, nauseating taste of blood. True, we are innocent, we are the victims, robbed, betrayed, outraged; and yet for all that, or precisely because of

55

it, the flame of evil glowers in our moral indignation. It must be so, for it is necessary that someone should feel indignant, that someone should let himself be the sword of judgment wielded by fate. Evil calls for expiation, otherwise the wicked will destroy the world utterly, or the good suffocate in their rage which they cannot vent, and in either case no good will come of it.

When evil breaks at any point into the order of things, our whole circle of psychic protection is disrupted. Action inevitably calls up reaction, and, in the matter of destructiveness, this turns out to be just as bad as the crime, and possibly even worse, because the evil must be exterminated root and branch. In order to escape the contaminating touch of evil we need a proper *rite de sortie*, a solemn admission of guilt by judge, hangman, and public, followed by an act of expiation.

The terrible things that have happened in Germany, and the moral downfall of a "nation of eighty millions," are a blow aimed at all Europeans. (We used to be able to relegate such things to "Asia!") The fact that one member of the European family could sink to the level of the concentration camp throws a dubious light on all the others. Who are we to imagine that "it couldn't happen here"? We have only to multiply the population of Switzerland by twenty to become a nation of eighty millions, and our public intelligence and morality would then automatically be divided by twenty in consequence of the devastating moral and psychic effects of living together in huge masses. Such a state of things provides the basis for collective crime, and it is then really a miracle if the crime is not committed. Do we seriously believe that *we* would have been immune? We, who have so many traitors and political psychopaths in our midst? It has filled us with horror to realize all that man is capable of, and of which, therefore, we too are capable. Since then a terrible doubt about humanity, and about ourselves, gnaws at our hearts.

Nevertheless, it should be clear to everyone that such a state of degradation can come about only under certain conditions. The most important of these is the accumulation of urban, industrialized masses—of people torn from the soil, engaged in one-sided employment, and lacking every healthy instinct, even that of self-preservation. Loss of the instinct of self-preservation can

56

be measured in terms of dependence on the State, which is a bad symptom. Dependence on the State means that everybody relies on everybody else (= State) instead of on himself. Every man hangs on to the next and enjoys a false feeling of security, for one is still hanging in the air even when hanging in the company of ten thousand other people. The only difference is that one is no longer aware of one's own insecurity. The increasing dependence on the State is anything but a healthy symptom; it means that the whole nation is in a fair way to becoming a herd of sheep, constantly relying on a shepherd to drive them into good pastures. The shepherd's staff soon becomes a rod of iron, and the shepherds turn into wolves. What a distressing sight it was to see the whole of Germany heave a sigh of relief when a megalomaniac psychopath proclaimed, "I take over the responsibility!" Any man who still possesses the instinct of self-preservation knows perfectly well that only a swindler would offer to relieve him of responsibility, for surely no one in his senses would dream of taking responsibility for the existence of another. The man who promises everything is sure to fulfil nothing, and everyone who promises too much is in danger of using evil means in order to carry out his promises, and is already on the road to perdition. The steady growth of the Welfare State is no doubt a very fine thing from one point of view, but from another it is a doubtful blessing, as it robs people of their individual responsibility and turns them into infants and sheep. Besides this, there is the danger that the capable will simply be exploited by the irresponsible, as happened on a huge scale in Germany. The citizen's instinct of self-preservation should be safeguarded at all costs, for, once a man is cut off from the nourishing roots of instinct, he becomes the shuttlecock of every wind that blows. He is then no better than a sick animal, demoralized and degenerate, and nothing short of a catastrophe can bring him back to health.

I own that in saying all this I feel rather like the prophet who, according to Josephus, lifted up his voice in lamentation over the city as the Romans laid siege to Jerusalem. It proved not the slightest use to the city, and a stone missile from a Roman ballista put an end to the prophet.

With the best will in the world we cannot build a paradise on earth, and even if we could, in a very short time we would

57

have degenerated in every way. We would take delight in destroying our paradise, and then, just as foolishly, marvel at what we had done. Moreover, if we happened to be a "nation of eighty millions" we would be convinced that the "others" were to blame, and our self-confidence would be at such a low ebb that we would not even think of shouldering the responsibility or taking the blame for anything.

This is a pathological, demoralized, and mentally abnormal condition: one side of us does things which the other (so-called decent) side prefers to ignore. This side is in a perpetual state of defence against real and supposed accusations. In reality the chief accuser is not outside, but the judge who dwells in our own hearts. Since this is nature's attempt to bring about a cure, it would be wiser not to persist too long in rubbing the noses of the Germans in their own abominations, lest we drown the voice of the accuser in their hearts—and also in our own hearts and those of our Allies. If only people could realize what an enrichment it is to find one's own guilt, what a sense of honour and spiritual dignity! But nowhere does there seem to be a glimmering of this insight. Instead, we hear only of attempts to shift the blame on to others—"no one will admit to having been a Nazi." The Germans were never wholly indifferent to the impression they made on the outside world. They resented disapproval and hated even to be criticized. Inferiority feelings make people touchy and lead to compensatory efforts to impress. As a result, the German thrusts himself forward and seeks to curry favour, or "German efficiency" is demonstrated with such aplomb that it leads to a reign of terror and the shooting of hostages. The German no longer thinks of these things as murder, for he is lost in considerations of his own prestige. Inferiority feelings are usually a sign of inferior feeling—which is not just a play on words. All the intellectual and technological achievements in the world cannot make up for inferiority in the matter of feeling. The pseudo-scientific race-theories with which it was dolled up did not make the extermination of the Jews any more acceptable, and neither do falsifications of history make a wrong policy appear any more trustworthy.

This spectacle recalls the figure of what Nietzsche so aptly calls the "pale criminal," who in reality shows all the signs of hysteria. He simply will not and cannot admit that he is what he is; he cannot endure his own guilt, just as he could not help incurring it. He will stoop to every kind of self-deception if only he can escape the sight of himself. It is true that this happens everywhere, but nowhere does it appear to be such a national characteristic as in Germany. I am by no means the first to have been struck by the inferiority feelings of the Germans. What did Goethe, Heine, and Nietzsche have to say about their countrymen? A feeling of inferiority does not in the least mean that it is unjustified. Only, the inferiority does not refer to that side of the personality, or to the function, in which it visibly appears, but to an inferiority which none the less really exists even though only dimly suspected. This condition can easily lead to an hysterical dissociation of the personality, which consists essentially in one hand not knowing what the other is doing, in wanting to jump over one's own shadow, and in looking for everything dark, inferior, and culpable *in others.* Hence the hysteric always complains of being surrounded by people who are incapable of appreciating him and who are activated only by bad motives; by inferior mischief-makers, a crowd of submen who should be exterminated neck and crop so that the Superman can live on his high level of perfection. The very fact that his thinking and feeling proceed along these lines is clear proof of inferiority in action. Therefore all hysterical people are compelled to torment others, because they are unwilling to hurt themselves by admitting their own inferiority. But since nobody can jump out of his skin and be rid of himself, they stand in their own way everywhere as their own evil spirit—and that is what we call an hysterical neurosis.

All these pathological features—complete lack of insight into one's own character, auto-erotic self-admiration and self-extenuation, denigration and terrorization of one's fellow men (how contemptuously Hitler spoke of his own people!), projection of the shadow, lying, falsification of reality, determination to impress by fair means or foul, bluffing and double-crossing—all these were united in the man who was diagnosed clinically as an hysteric, and whom a strange fate chose to be the political, moral, and religious spokesman of Germany for twelve years. Is this pure chance?

A more accurate diagnosis of Hitler's condition would be *pseudologia phantastica,* that form of hysteria which is characterized by a peculiar talent for believing one's own lies. For a short spell, such people usually meet with astounding success, and for that reason are socially dangerous. Nothing has such a convincing effect as a lie one invents and believes oneself, or an evil deed or intention whose righteousness one regards as self-evident. At any rate they carry far more conviction than the good man and the good deed, or even than the wicked man and his purely wicked deed. Hitler's theatrical, obviously hysterical gestures struck all foreigners (with a few amazing exceptions) as purely ridiculous. When I saw him with my own eyes, he suggested a psychic scarecrow (with a broomstick for an outstretched arm) rather than a human being. It is also difficult to understand how his ranting speeches, delivered in shrill, grating, womanish tones, could have made such an impression. But the German people would never have been taken in and carried away so completely if this figure had not been a reflected image of the collective German hysteria. It is not without serious misgivings that one ventures to pin the label of "psychopathic inferiority" on to a whole nation, and yet, heaven knows, it is the only explanation which could in any way account for the effect this scarecrow had on the masses. A sorry lack of education, conceit that bordered on madness, a very mediocre intelligence combined with the hysteric's cunning and the power fantasies of an adolescent, were written all over this demagogue's face. His gesticulations were all put on, devised by an hysterical mind intent only on making an impression. He behaved in public like a man living in his own biography, in this case as the sombre, daemonic "man of iron" of popular fiction, the ideal of an infantile public whose knowledge of the world is derived from the deified heroes of trashy films. These personal observations led me to conclude at the time (1937) that, when the final catastrophe came, it would be far greater and bloodier than I had previously supposed. For this theatrical hysteric and transparent impostor was not strutting about on a small stage, but was riding the armoured divisions of the Wehrmacht, with all the weight of German heavy industry behind him. Encountering only slight and in any case ineffective opposition from within, the nation of eighty millions crowded into the circus to witness its own destruction.

Among Hitler's closest associates, Goebbels and Göring stand out as equally striking figures. Göring is the good fellow and *bon vivant* type of cheat, who takes in the simple-minded with his jovial air of respectability; Goebbels, a no-less-sinister and dangerous character, is the typical *Kaffeehausliterat* and card-sharper, handicapped and at the same time branded by nature. Any one partner in this unholy trinity should have been enough to make any man whose instincts were not warped cross himself three times. But what in fact happened? Hitler was exalted to the skies; there were even theologians who looked upon him as the Saviour. Göring was popular on account of his weaknesses; few people would believe his crimes. Goebbels was tolerated because many people think that lying is inseparable from success, and that success justifies everything. Three of these types at one time were really the limit, and one is at a loss to imagine how anything quite so monstrous ever came to power. But we must not forget that we are judging from today, from a knowledge of the events which led to the catastrophe. Our judgment would certainly be very different had our information stopped short at 1933 or 1934. At that time, in Germany as well as in Italy, there were not a few things that appeared plausible and seemed to speak in favour of the regime. An undeniable piece of evidence in this respect was the disappearance of the unemployed, who used to tramp the German highroads in their hundreds of thousands. And after the stagnation and decay of the post-war years, the refreshing wind that blew through the two countries was a tempting sign of hope. Meanwhile, the whole of Europe looked on at this spectacle like Mr. Chamberlain, who was prepared at most for a heavy shower. But it is just this extreme speciousness that is the peculiar genius of *pseudologia phantastica*, and Mussolini also had a touch of it (kept within bounds, however, while his brother Arnaldo was alive). It introduces its plans in the most innocent way in the world, finding the most appropriate words and the most plausible arguments, and there is nothing to show that its intentions are bad from the start. They may even be good, genuinely good. In the case of Mussolini, for instance, it might be difficult to draw a definite line between black and white. Where *pseudologia* is at work one can never be sure that the intention to deceive is the principal motive. Quite often the "great plan" plays the leading role, and it is only when it comes to the ticklish question of

61

bringing this plan into reality that every opportunity is exploited and any means is good enough, on the principle that "the end justifies the means." In other words, things only become dangerous when the pathological liar is taken seriously by a wider public. Like Faust, he is bound to make a pact with the devil and thus slips off the straight path. It is even possible that this is more or less what happened to Hitler—let us give him the benefit of the doubt! But the infamies of his book, once it is shorn of its *Schwabinger* [3] brand of bombast, make one suspicious, and one cannot help wondering if the evil spirit had not already taken possession of this man long before he seized power. Round about 1936, many people in Germany were asking themselves the same question; they expressed fears that the Führer might fall a victim to "evil influences," he dabbled too much in "black magic," etc. Clearly these misgivings came much too late; but even so, it is just conceivable that Hitler himself may have had good intentions at first, and only succumbed to the use of the wrong means, or the misuse of his means, in the course of his development.

But I should like to emphasize above all that it is part and parcel of the pathological liar's make-up to be plausible. Therefore it is no easy matter, even for experienced people, to form an opinion, particularly while the plan is still apparently in the idealistic stage. It is then quite impossible to foresee how things are likely to develop, and Mr. Chamberlain's "give-it-a-chance" attitude seems to be the only policy. The overwhelming majority of the Germans were just as much in the dark as people abroad, and quite naturally fell an easy prey to Hitler's speeches, so artfully attuned to German (and not only German) taste.

Although we may be able to understand why the Germans were misled in the first place, the almost total absence of any reaction is quite incomprehensible. Were there not army commanders who could have ordered their troops to do anything they pleased? Why then was the reaction totally lacking? I can only explain this as the outcome of a peculiar state of mind, a passing or chronic disposition which, in an individual, we call hysteria.

As I cannot take it for granted that the layman knows exactly what is meant by "hysteria," I had better explain that the "hys-

3 [Schwabing is the bohemian quarter of Munich.—EDITORS.]

terical" disposition forms a sub-division of what are known as "psychopathic inferiorities." This term by no means implies that the individual or the nation is "inferior" in every respect, but only that there is a place of least resistance, a peculiar instability, which exists independently of all the other qualities. An hysterical disposition means that the opposites inherent in every psyche, and especially those affecting character, are further apart than in normal people. This greater distance produces a higher energic tension, which accounts for the undeniable energy and drive of the Germans. On the other hand, the greater distance between the opposites produces inner contradictions, conflicts of conscience, disharmonies of character—in short, everything we see in Goethe's Faust. Nobody but a German could ever have devised such a figure, it is so intrinsically, so infinitely German. In Faust we see the same "hungering for the infinite" born of inner contradiction and dichotomy, the same eschatological expectation of the Great Fulfilment. In him we experience the loftiest flight of the mind and the descent into the depths of guilt and darkness, and still worse, a fall so low that Faust sinks to the level of a mountebank and wholesale murderer as the outcome of his pact with the devil. Faust, too, is split and sets up "evil" outside himself in the shape of Mephistopheles, to serve as an alibi in case of need. He likewise "knows nothing of what has happened," i.e., what the devil did to Philemon and Baucis. We never get the impression that he has real insight or suffers genuine remorse. His avowed and unavowed worship of success stands in the way of any moral reflection throughout, obscuring the ethical conflict, so that Faust's moral personality remains misty. He never attains the character of reality: he is not a real human being and cannot become one (at least not in this world). He remains the German idea of a human being, and therefore an image—somewhat overdone and distorted—of the average German.

The essence of hysteria is a systematic dissociation, a loosening of the opposites which normally are held firmly together. It may even go to the length of a splitting of the personality, a condition in which quite literally one hand no longer knows what the other is doing. As a rule there is amazing ignorance of the shadow; the hysteric is only aware of his good motives, and when the bad ones can no longer be denied he becomes the unscrupu-

63

lous Superman and *Herrenmensch* who fancies he is ennobled by the magnitude of his aim.

Ignorance of one's other side creates great inner insecurity. One does not really know who one is; one feels inferior somewhere and yet does not wish to know where the inferiority lies, with the result that a new inferiority is added to the original one. This sense of insecurity is the source of the hysteric's prestige psychology, of his need to make an impression, to flaunt his merits and insist on them, of his insatiable thirst for recognition, admiration, adulation, and longing to be loved. It is the cause of that loud-mouthed arrogance, uppishness, insolence, and tactlessness by which so many Germans, who at home grovel like dogs, win a bad reputation for their countrymen abroad. Insecurity is also responsible for their tragic lack of civic courage, criticized by Bismarck (one need only recall the pitiable role of the German generals).

The lack of reality, so striking in Faust, produces a corresponding lack of realism in the German. He merely talks of it, boasting of his "ice-cold" realism, which in itself is enough to expose his hysteria. His realism is nothing but a pose, a stage-realism. He merely acts the part of one who has a sense of reality, but what does he actually want to do? He wants to conquer the world in spite of the whole world. Of course, he has no idea how it can be done. But at least he might know that the enterprise had failed once before. Unfortunately a plausible reason, that explains away the failure by means of lies, is immediately invented and believed. How many Germans were taken in by the legend of the "stab in the back" in 1918? And how many "stab in the back" legends are floating around today? Believing one's own lies when the wish is father to the lie is a well-known hysterical symptom and a distinct sign of inferiority. One would have thought that the bloodbath of the first World War would have been enough, but not a bit of it; glory, conquest, and bloodthirstiness acted like a smoke-screen on the German mind, so that reality, only dimly perceived at best, was completely blotted out. In an individual we call this sort of thing an hysterical twilight-state. When a whole nation finds itself in this condition it will follow a mediumistic Führer over the housetops with a sleep-walker's assurance, only to land in the street with a broken back.

64

Supposing we Swiss had started such a war and had thrown all our experience, all warnings and all our knowledge of the world to the winds as blindly as the Germans, and had finally gone to the length of establishing an original edition of Buchenwald in our country. We should no doubt feel very disagreeably surprised if a foreigner declared that the Swiss were one and all completely mad. No reasonable person would be surprised at such a verdict, but can we say it about Germany? I wonder what the Germans themselves think. All I know is that at the time of the censorship in Switzerland we were not permitted to say these things aloud, and now it seems we cannot say them out of consideration for Germany which is laid so low. When on earth, I should like to ask, may one venture to form an opinion of one's own? To my mind, the history of the last twelve years is the case-chart of an hysterical patient. The truth should not be withheld from him, for when the doctor makes a diagnosis he does so as part of his effort to find the remedy, and not in order to hurt, degrade, or insult the sufferer. A neurosis or a neurotic disposition is not a disgrace, it is a handicap, and sometimes merely a *façon de parler*. It is not a fatal disease, but it does grow worse to the degree that one is determined to ignore it. When I say that the Germans are psychically ill it is surely kinder than saying that they are criminals. I have no wish to irritate the notorious sensitiveness of the hysteric, but there comes a time when we can no longer afford to gloss over all the painful symptoms and to help the patient forget what has happened, merely in order that his pathological condition should remain undisturbed. I would not like to insult the healthy-minded and decent German by suspecting him of being a coward who runs away from his own image. We should do him the honour of treating him like a man and telling him the truth, and not conceal from him that our soul is cut to the quick by the terrible things that happened in his country and were perpetrated by the Germans in Europe. We are hurt and indignant and have no particular feelings of loving-kindness—nor can any amount of determination and will-power twist these sentiments into a Christian "love of your neighbour." For the sake of the healthy-minded and decent Germans one should not attempt to do so; they would surely prefer the truth to insulting forbearance.

Hysteria is never cured by hushing up the truth, whether in

65

an individual or in a nation. But can we say that a whole nation is hysterical? We can say it as much or as little of a nation as of an individual. Even the craziest person is not completely crazy; quite a number of his functions are still normal, and there may even be times when he himself is fairly normal too. This is even truer of hysteria, where there is really nothing wrong except exaggerations and excesses on the one hand, and weakness or temporary paralysis of normal functions on the other. In spite of his psychopathic condition the hysteric is very nearly normal. We may therefore expect many parts of the psychic body-politic to be entirely normal even though the over-all picture can only be described as hysterical.

The Germans undoubtedly have their own peculiar psychology which distinguishes them from their neighbours, in spite of the many human qualities which they share with all mankind. Have they not demonstrated to the world that they consider themselves the *Herrenvolk,* with the right to disregard every human scruple? They have labelled other nations inferior and done their best to exterminate them.

In view of these terrible facts, it is a mere bagatelle to turn the tables on the *Herrenvolk* and apply the diagnosis of inferiority to the murderer instead of the murdered, while remaining fully conscious that one is injuring all those Germans who suffered their nation's tribulation with open eyes. It does indeed hurt one to hurt others. But, as Europeans—a brotherhood which includes the Germans—we are wounded, and if we wound in return it is not with the intention of torturing but, as I said earlier, of discovering the truth. As in the case of collective guilt, the diagnosis of its mental condition extends to the whole nation, and indeed to the whole of Europe, whose mental condition for some time past has hardly been normal. Whether we like it or not we are bound to ask: What is wrong with our art, that most delicate of all instruments for reflecting the national psyche? How are we to explain the blatantly pathological element in modern painting? Atonal music? The far-reaching influence of Joyce's fathomless *Ulysses?* Here we already have the germ of what was to become a political reality in Germany.

The European, or rather the white man in general, is scarcely in a position to judge of his own state of mind. He is too deeply involved. I had always wanted to see Europeans through other eyes, and eventually I was able, on my many journeys, to establish sufficiently close relationships with non-Europeans to see the European through their eyes. The white man is nervous, restless, hurried, unstable, and (in the eyes of non-Europeans) possessed by the craziest ideas, in spite of his energy and gifts which give him the feeling of being infinitely superior. The crimes he has committed against the coloured races are legion, though obviously this is no justification for any fresh crime, just as the individual is no better for being in a vast company of bad people. Primitives dread the sharply focussed stare in the eye of the European, which seems to them like the evil eye. A Pueblo chieftain once confided to me that he thought all Americans (the only white men he knew) were crazy, and the reasons he gave for this view sounded exactly like a description of people who were possessed. Well, perhaps we are. For the first time since the dawn of history we have succeeded in swallowing the whole of primitive animism into ourselves, and with it the spirit that animated nature. Not only were the gods dragged down from their planetary spheres and transformed into chthonic demons, but, under the influence of scientific enlightenment, even this band of demons, which at the time of Paracelsus still frolicked happily in mountains and woods, in rivers and human dwelling-places, was reduced to a miserable remnant and finally vanished altogether. From time immemorial, nature was always filled with spirit. Now, for the first time, we are living in a lifeless nature bereft of gods. No one will deny the important role which the powers of the human psyche, personified as "gods," played in the past. The mere act of enlightenment may have destroyed the spirits of nature, but not the psychic factors that correspond to them, such as suggestibility, lack of criticism, fearfulness, propensity to superstition and prejudice—in short, all those qualities which make possession possible. Even though nature is depsychized, the psychic conditions which breed demons are as actively at work as ever. The demons have not really disappeared but have merely taken on another form: they have become unconscious psychic forces. This process of reabsorption went hand in hand with an increasing inflation of the ego, which became more and more evident after the sixteenth century. Finally we even began to be aware of the psyche, and, as history shows, the discovery of the unconscious was a particularly painful episode. Just when people were congratulating themselves on having abolished all spooks, it turned out that instead of haunting the attic or old ruins the spooks were flitting about in the heads of apparently normal Europeans. Tyrannical, obsessive, intoxicating ideas and delusions were abroad everywhere, and people began to believe the most absurd things, just as the possessed do.

The phenomenon we have witnessed in Germany was nothing less than the first outbreak of epidemic insanity, an irruption of the unconscious into what seemed to be a tolerably well-ordered world. A whole nation, as well as countless millions belonging to other nations, were swept into the blood-drenched madness of a war of extermination. No one knew what was happening to him, least of all the Germans, who allowed themselves to be driven to the slaughterhouse by their leading psychopaths like hypnotized sheep. Maybe the Germans were predestined to this fate, for they showed the least resistance to the mental contagion that threatened every European. But their peculiar gifts might also have enabled them to be the very people to draw helpful conclusions from the prophetic example of Nietzsche. Nietzsche was German to the marrow of his bones, even to the abstruse symbolism of his madness. It was the psychopath's weakness that prompted him to play with the "blond beast" and the "Superman." It was certainly not the healthy elements in the German nation that led to the triumph of these pathological fantasies on a scale never known before. The weakness of the German character, like Nietzsche's, proved to be fertile soil for hysterical fantasies, though it must be remembered that Nietzsche himself not only criticized the German Philistine very freely but laid himself open to attack on a broad front. Here again the Germans had a priceless opportunity for self-knowledge—and let it slip. And what could they not have learned from the suet-and-syrup of Wagner!

Nevertheless, with the calamitous founding of the Reich in 1871, the devil stole a march on the Germans, dangling before them the tempting bait of power, aggrandizement, national arrogance. Thus they were led to imitate their prophets and to take their words literally, but not to understand them. And so it was that the Germans allowed themselves to be deluded by these disastrous fantasies and succumbed to the age-old temptations

68

of Satan, instead of turning to their abundant spiritual potenti-
alities, which, because of the greater tension between the inner
opposites, would have stood them in good stead. But, their Christianity forgotten, they sold their souls to technology, exchanged
morality for cynicism, and dedicated their highest aspirations to
the forces of destruction. Certainly everybody else is doing much
the same thing, but even so there really are chosen people who
have no right to do such things because they should be striving
for higher treasures. At any rate the Germans are not among
those who may enjoy power and possessions with impunity. Just
think for a moment what anti-Semitism means for the German:
he is trying to use others as a scapegoat for his own greatest
fault! This symptom alone should have told him that he had
got on to a hopelessly wrong track.

After the last World War the world should have begun to
reflect, and above all Germany, which is the nerve-centre of
Europe. But the spirit turned negative, neglected the decisive
questions, and sought solutions in its own negation. How different it was at the time of the Reformation! Then the spirit of
Germany rose manfully to the needs of Christendom, though
the answer—as we might expect from the German tension of
opposites—was somewhat too extreme. But at least this spirit did
not shrink from its own problems. Goethe, too, was a prophet
when he held up before his people the example of Faust's pact
with the devil and the murder of Philemon and Baucis. If, as
Burckhardt says, Faust strikes a chord in every German soul,
this chord has certainly gone on ringing. We hear it echoing
in Nietzsche's Superman, the amoral worshipper of instinct,
whose God is dead, and who presumes to be God himself, or
rather a demon "six thousand feet beyond good and evil." And
where has the feminine side, the soul, disappeared to in Nietzsche? Helen has vanished in Hades, and Eurydice will never
return. Already we behold the fateful travesty of the denied
Christ: the sick prophet is himself the Crucified, and, going back
still further, the dismembered Dionysus-Zagreus. The raving
prophet carries us back to the long-forgotten past: he had heard
the call of destiny in the shrill whistling of the hunter, the god
of the rustling forests, of drunken ecstasy, and of the berserkers
who were possessed by the spirits of wild animals.

While Nietzsche was prophetically responding to the schism

of the Christian world with the art of thinking, his brother in spirit, Richard Wagner, was doing the same thing with the art of music. Germanic prehistory comes surging up, thunderous and stupefying, to fill the gaping breach in the Church. Wagner salved his conscience with *Parsifal*, for which Nietzsche could never forgive him, but the Castle of the Grail vanished into an unknown land. The message was not heard and the omen went unheeded. Only the orgiastic frenzy caught on and spread like an epidemic. Wotan the storm-god had conquered. Ernst Jünger sensed that very clearly: in his book *On the Marble Cliffs* a wild huntsman comes into the land, bringing with him a wave of possession greater than anything known even in the Middle Ages. Nowhere did the European spirit speak more plainly than it did in Germany, and nowhere was it more tragically misunderstood.

Now Germany has suffered the consequences of the pact with the devil, she has experienced madness and is torn in pieces like Zagreus, she has been ravished by the berserkers of her god Wotan, been cheated of her soul for the sake of gold and world-mastery, and defiled by the scum rising from the lowest depths.

The Germans must understand why the whole world is outraged, for our expectations had been so different. Everybody was unanimous in recognizing their gifts and their efficiency, and nobody doubted that they were capable of great things. The disappointment was all the more bitter. But the fate of Germany should not mislead Europeans into nursing the illusion that the whole world's wickedness is localized in Germany. They should realize that the German catastrophe was only one crisis in the general European sickness. Long before the Hitler era, in fact before the first World War, there were symptoms of the mental change taking place in Europe. The medieval picture of the world was breaking up and the metaphysical authority that ruled it was fast disappearing, only to reappear in man. Did not Nietzsche announce that God was dead and that his heir was the Superman, that doomed rope-dancer and fool? It is an immutable psychological law that when a projection has come to an end it always returns to its origin. So when somebody hits on the singular idea that God is dead, or does not exist at all, the psychic God-image, which is a dynamic part of the psyche's structure, finds its way back into the subject and produces a condi-

70

tion of "God-Almightiness," that is to say all those qualities which are peculiar to fools and madmen and therefore lead to catastrophe.

This, then, is the great problem that faces the whole of Christianity: where now is the sanction for goodness and justice, which was once anchored in metaphysics? Is it really only brute force that decides everything? Is the ultimate authority only the will of whatever man happens to be in power? Had Germany been victorious, one might almost have believed that this was the last word. But as the "thousand-year Reich" of violence and infamy lasted only a few years before it collapsed in ruins, we might be disposed to learn the lesson that there are other, equally powerful forces at work which in the end destroy all that is violent and unjust, and that consequently it does not pay to build on false principles. But unfortunately, as history shows, things do not always turn out so reasonably in this world of ours.

"God-Almightiness" does not make man divine, it merely fills him with arrogance and arouses everything evil in him. It produces a diabolical caricature of man, and this inhuman mask is so unendurable, such a torture to wear, that he tortures others. He is split in himself, a prey to inexplicable contradictions. Here we have the picture of the hysterical state of mind, of Nietzsche's "pale criminal." Fate has confronted every German with his inner counterpart: Faust is face to face with Mephistopheles and can no longer say, "So that was the essence of the brute!" He must confess instead: "That was my other side, my *alter ego,* my all too palpable shadow which can no longer be denied."

This is not the fate of Germany alone, but of all Europe. We must all open our eyes to the shadow who looms behind contemporary man. We have no need to hold up the devil's mask before the Germans. The facts speak a plainer language, and anyone who does not understand it is simply beyond help. As to what should be done about this terrifying apparition, everyone must work this out for himself. It is indeed no small matter to know of one's own guilt and one's own evil, and there is certainly nothing to be gained by losing sight of one's shadow. When we are conscious of our guilt we are in a more favourable position—we can at least hope to change and improve ourselves. As we know, anything that remains in the unconscious

71

is incorrigible; psychological corrections can be made only in consciousness. Consciousness of guilt can therefore act as a powerful moral stimulus. In every treatment of neurosis the discovery of the shadow is indispensable, otherwise nothing changes. In this respect, I rely on those parts of the German body-politic which have remained sound to draw conclusions from the facts. Without guilt, unfortunately, there can be no psychic maturation and no widening of the spiritual horizon. Was it not Meister Eckhart who said: "For this reason God is willing to bear the brunt of sins and often winks at them, mostly sending them to people for whom he has prepared some high destiny. See! Who was dearer to our Lord or more intimate with him than his apostles? Not one of them but fell into mortal sin, and all were mortal sinners." [4]

Where sin is great, "grace doth much more abound." Such an experience brings about an inner transformation, and this is infinitely more important than political and social reforms which are all valueless in the hands of people who are not at one with themselves. This is a truth which we are forever forgetting, because our eyes are fascinated by the conditions around us and riveted on them instead of examining our own heart and conscience. Every demagogue exploits this human weakness when he points with the greatest possible outcry to all the things that are wrong in the outside world. But the principal and indeed the only thing that is wrong with the world is man.

If the Germans today are having a hard time of it outwardly, fate has at least given them a unique opportunity of turning their eyes inward to the inner man. In this way they might make amends for a sin of omission of which our whole civilization is guilty. Everything possible has been done for the outside world: science has been refined to an unimaginable extent, technical achievement has reached an almost uncanny degree of perfection. But what of man, who is expected to administer all these blessings in a reasonable way? He has simply been taken for granted. No one has stopped to consider that neither morally nor psychologically is he in any way adapted to such changes. As blithely as any child of nature he sets about enjoying these dangerous playthings, completely oblivious of the shadow lurk-

---

4 *Works*, trans. by Evans, II, pp. 18–19.

ing behind him, ready to seize them in its greedy grasp and turn them against a still infantile and unconscious humanity. And who has had a more immediate experience of this feeling of helplessness and abandonment to the powers of darkness than the German who fell into the clutches of the Germans?

If collective guilt could only be understood and accepted, a great step forward would have been taken. But this alone is no cure, just as no neurotic is cured by mere understanding. The question remains: How am I to live with this shadow? What attitude is required if I am to be able to live in spite of evil? In order to find valid answers to these questions a complete spiritual renewal is needed. And this cannot be given gratis, each man must strive to achieve it for himself. Neither can old formulas which once had a value be brought into force again. The eternal truths cannot be transmitted mechanically; in every epoch they must be born anew from the human psyche.

6

Epilogue

Germany has set the world a tremendous problem, a problem that has to be considered from many angles. The psychological aspect is only one of its many facets. As a psychologist, I am naturally inclined to think it an important facet, but I must leave it to my reader to form his own opinion on this point. My professional concern with the psychology of the unconscious often brings to light things which are still hidden from consciousness but exist in embryonic form; and these contents are ready to break through into consciousness long before the individual has any idea of what his psyche holds in store for him. I had an inkling of what was brewing in the unconscious nearly thirty years ago, for I had Germans among my patients. As early as 1918 I wrote:

As the Christian view of the world loses its authority, the more menacingly will the "blond beast" be heard prowling about in its underground prison, ready at any moment to burst out with devastating consequences.[1]

It hardly requires an Oedipus to guess what is meant by the "blond beast." I had an idea, however, that this "blond beast" was not restricted to Germany, but stood for the primitive European in general, who was gradually coming to the surface as a result of ever-increasing mass organization. In the same article I went on to say:

Even the primitive's distrust of the neighbouring tribe, which we thought we had long ago outgrown thanks to our global organizations, has come back again in this war, swollen to gigantic propor-

---

[1] "The Role of the Unconscious," in *Civilization in Transition*, par. 17.

tions. It is no longer a matter of burning down the neighbouring village, or of making a few heads roll: whole countries are devastated, millions are slaughtered. The enemy nation is stripped of every shred of decency, and our own faults appear in others, fantastically magnified. Where are the superior minds, capable of reflection, today? If they exist at all, nobody heeds them: instead there is a general running amok, a universal fatality against whose compelling sway the individual is powerless to defend himself. And yet this collective phenomenon is the fault of the individual as well, for nations are made up of individuals. Therefore the individual must consider by what means he can counter the evil. Our rationalistic attitude leads us to believe that we can work wonders with international organizations, legislation, and other well-meant devices. But in reality only a change in the attitude of the individual can bring about a renewal in the spirit of the nations. Everything begins with the individual. There are well-meaning theologians and humanitarians who want to break the power principle—in others. We must begin by breaking it in ourselves. Then the thing becomes credible.[2]

While the first World War was still in progress, I wrote an essay that first appeared in French, which I enlarged and published as a book in Germany in 1928.[3] Dealing among other things with the subject of mass psychology, I said:

It is a notorious fact that the morality of society as a whole is in inverse ratio to its size; the greater the aggregation of individuals, the more the individual factors are blotted out, and with them morality, which depends entirely on the moral sense of the individual and on the freedom necessary for this. Hence every man is, in a certain sense, unconsciously a worse man when he is in society than when acting alone; for he is carried by society and to that extent relieved of his individual responsibility. Any large company composed of wholly admirable persons has the morality and intelligence of an unwieldy, stupid, and violent animal. The bigger the organization, the more unavoidable is its immorality and blind stupidity. (*Senatus bestia, senatores boni viri.*) Society, by automatically stressing all the collective qualities in its individual representatives, puts a premium on mediocrity, on everything that settles down to vegetate in an easy, irresponsible way. Individuality will inevitably be driven to the wall.

[2] Ibid., pars. 45f.
[3] "The Structure of the Unconscious," expanded into "The Relations between the Ego and the Unconscious." Both in *Two Essays on Analytical Psychology.*

. . . Without freedom there can be no morality. Our admiration for great organizations dwindles when once we become aware of the other side of the wonder: the tremendous piling up and accentuation of all that is primitive in man, and the unavoidable destruction of his individuality in the interests of the monstrosity that every great organization in fact is. The man of today, who resembles more or less the collective ideal, has made his heart into a den of murderers, as can easily be proved by the analysis of his unconscious, even though he himself is not in the least disturbed by this fact. And in so far as he is normally adapted to his environment, it is true that the greatest infamy on the part of his group will not disturb him, so long as the majority of his fellows steadfastly believe in the exalted morality of their social organization.[4]

In the same essay I uttered the almost banal truth: "The best, just because it is the best, holds the seed of evil, and there is nothing so bad but good can come of it."[5] I lay particular stress on this sentence, because it always put me in a mood of caution when I had to judge of any particular manifestation of the unconscious. The contents of the collective unconscious, the archetypes, with which we are concerned in any occurrence of psychic mass-phenomena, are always bipolar: they have both a positive and a negative side. Whenever an archetype appears things become critical, and it is impossible to foresee what turn they will take. As a rule this depends on the way consciousness reacts to the situation. During a collective manifestation of archetypes there is always a great danger of a mass movement, and a catastrophe can be avoided only if the effect of the archetype can be intercepted and assimilated by a sufficiently large majority of individuals. At the very least there must be a certain number of individuals who are still capable of making their influence felt.

In February 1933, lecturing in Cologne and Essen, I said:

The decidedly individualistic trend of these latest developments is counterbalanced by a compensatory reversion to the collective man, whose authority at present is the sheer weight of the masses. No wonder that nowadays there is a feeling of catastrophe in the air, as though an avalanche had broken loose which nothing can stop. The

[4] *Two Essays,* par. 240.
[5] Ibid., par. 289.

collective man threatens to stifle the individual man, on whose sense of responsibility everything valuable in mankind ultimately depends. The mass as such is always anonymous and always irresponsible. So-called leaders are the inevitable symptoms of a mass movement. The true leaders of mankind are always those who are capable of self-reflection, and who relieve the dead weight of the masses at least of their own weight, consciously holding aloof from the blind momentum of the mass in movement.

But who can resist this all-engulfing force of attraction, when each man clings to the next and each drags the other with him? Only one who is firmly rooted not only in the outside world but also in the world within.

Small and hidden is the door that leads inward, and the entrance is barred by countless prejudices, mistaken assumptions, and fears. Always one wishes to hear of grand political and economic schemes, the very things that have landed every nation in a morass. Therefore it sounds grotesque when anyone speaks of hidden doors, dreams, and a world within. What has this vapid idealism got to do with gigantic economic programmes, with the so-called problems of reality?

But I speak not to nations, only to the individual few, for whom it goes without saying that cultural values do not drop down like manna from heaven, but are created by the hands of individuals. If things go wrong in the world, this is because something is wrong with the individual, because something is wrong with me. Therefore, if I am sensible, I shall put myself right first. For this I need—because outside authority no longer means anything to me—a knowledge of the innermost foundations of my being, in order that I may base myself firmly on the eternal facts of the human psyche.[6]

In the Terry Lectures, which I gave at Yale University in 1937, I said:

We can never be sure that a new idea will not seize either upon ourselves or upon our neighbours. We know from modern as well as from ancient history that such ideas are often so strange, indeed so bizarre, that they fly in the face of reason. The fascination which is almost invariably connected with ideas of this sort produces a fanatical obsession, with the result that all dissenters, no matter how well-meaning or reasonable they are, get burnt alive or have their heads cut off or are disposed of in masses by the more modern machine-gun. We cannot even console ourselves with the thought that such things belong

[6] "The Meaning of Psychology for Modern Man," in C. G. Jung, The Collected Works, Vol. 10, Civilization in Transition. Routledge & Kegan Paul, 2nd edn, 1970.

to the remote past. Unfortunately they seem to belong not only to the present, but, quite particularly, to the future. *Homo homini lupus* is a sad yet eternal truism. There is indeed reason enough for man to be afraid of the impersonal forces lurking in his unconscious. We are blissfully unconscious of these forces because they never, or almost never, appear in our personal relations or under ordinary circumstances. But if people crowd together and form a mob, then the dynamisms of the collective man are let loose—beasts or demons that lie dormant in every person until he is part of a mob. Man in the mass sinks unconsciously to an inferior moral and intellectual level, to that level which is always there, below the threshold of consciousness, ready to break forth as soon as it is activated by the formation of a mass. . . .

The change of character brought about by the uprush of collective forces is amazing. A gentle and reasonable being can be transformed into a maniac or a savage beast. One is always inclined to lay the blame on external circumstances, but nothing could explode in us if it had not been already there. As a matter of fact, we are constantly living on the edge of a volcano, and there is, so far as we know, no way of protecting ourselves from a possible outburst that will destroy everybody within reach. It is certainly a good thing to preach reason and common sense, but what if you have a lunatic asylum for an audience or a crowd in a collective frenzy? There is not much difference between them because the madman and the mob are both moved by impersonal, overwhelming forces. . . .[7]

Now we behold the amazing spectacle of states taking over the age-old totalitarian claims of theocracy, which are inevitably accompanied by the suppression of free opinion. Once more we see people cutting each other's throats in support of childish theories of how to create paradise on earth. It is not very difficult to see that the powers of the underworld—not to say of hell—which in former times were more or less successfully chained up in a gigantic spiritual edifice where they could be of some use, are now creating, or trying to create, a State slavery and a State prison devoid of any mental or spiritual charm. There are not a few people nowadays who are convinced that mere human reason is not entirely up to the enormous task of putting a lid on the volcano. . . .

Look at all the incredible savagery going on in our so-called civilized world: it all comes from human beings and their mental condition! Look at the devilish engines of destruction! They are invented by completely innocuous gentlemen, reasonable, respectable citizens who are everything we could wish. And when the whole thing blows

[7] "Psychology and Religion," pars. 23ff.

up and an indescribable hell of devastation is let loose, nobody seems to be responsible. It simply happens, and yet it is all man-made. But since everybody is blindly convinced that he is nothing more than his own extremely unassuming and insignificant conscious self, which performs its duties decently and earns a moderate living, nobody is aware that this whole rationalistically organized conglomeration we call a state or a nation is driven on by a seemingly impersonal but terrifying power which nobody and nothing can check. This ghastly power is mostly explained as fear of the neighbouring nation, which is supposed to be possessed by a malevolent fiend. Since nobody is capable of recognizing just where and how much he himself is possessed and unconscious, he simply projects his own condition upon his neighbour, and thus it becomes a sacred duty to have the biggest guns and the most poisonous gas. The worst of it is that he is quite right. All one's neighbours are in the grip of some uncontrollable fear, just like oneself. In lunatic asylums it is a well-known fact that patients are far more dangerous when suffering from fear than when moved by rage or hatred.[8]

During the "phoney war," early in 1940, I published a German translation of these lectures. The book was published just in time to reach Germany, but was soon suppressed on account of the passages just quoted, and I myself figured on the Nazi black list. I was a "marked man." After the invasion of France the Gestapo destroyed all the French editions of my books they were able to lay their hands on.

I have been blamed in many quarters for allowing myself to speak of German "psychopathy." I am—and always was—of the opinion that the political mass movements of our time are psychic epidemics, in other words, *mass psychoses*. They are, as their inhuman concomitants show, abnormal mental phenomena, and I refuse to regard such things as normal, to say nothing of whitewashing them as excusable blunders. Murder is murder, and the fact that the whole German nation threw itself with all its might into the most infamous war of aggression in history is a crime that nothing can ever wipe out. It is true that very many individuals stood out against it, but they were a small minority. The behaviour of the Germans in general is abnormal; were it not so, we should long since have been ac-

[8] Ibid., pars. 83ff.

customed to look upon this form of war as the normal state of things.

Naturally there were plenty of reasons—political, social, economic, and historical—to drive the Germans to war, just as there are in the case of common murder. Every murderer has motives enough to spur him on, or the crime would never be committed. But, in addition to all this, a special psychic disposition is needed to bring matters to such a point. That is why there is such a thing as criminal psychology. Germany was suffering from a mass psychosis which was bound to lead to crime. But no psychosis ever appears out of the blue, it is always the result of a long-standing predisposition which we call a psychopathic inferiority. Nations have their own peculiar psychology, and in the same way they also have their own particular kind of psychopathology. It consists in the accumulation of a large number of abnormal features, the most striking of which is a suggestibility affecting the entire nation. No doubt there are special reasons for this too, otherwise it would not exist. But the existence of reasons does not do away either with the deed or its character. There are plenty of reasons for both crime and madness, but we do not on that account send our criminals and lunatics to recuperate at the seaside.

I should like to point out that the idea of speaking of mass psychoses did not suddenly occur to me after May 1945; I had done that long before and had given warnings of this tremendous danger, not once but many times. As early as 1916, before the United States entered the first World War, I wrote:

Is the present war supposed to be a war of economics? That is a neutral American "business-like" standpoint, that does not take the blood, tears, unprecedented deeds of infamy and great distress into account, and which completely ignores the fact that this war is really an *epidemic of madness*.[9]

Once this function [of the irrational] finds itself in the unconscious, it works unceasing havoc, like an incurable disease whose focus cannot be eradicated because it is invisible. Individual and nation alike are then compelled to live the irrational in their own

[9] In *Collected Papers on Analytical Psychology* (1917), p. 416.

lives, even devoting their loftiest ideals and their best wits to expressing its madness in the most perfect form.[10]

In a lecture given at the British Society for Psychical Research in 1919, I said:

If this animation [of the collective unconscious] is due to a complete breakdown of all conscious hopes and expectations, the danger arises that the unconscious may take the place of conscious reality. Such a state is morbid. We actually see something of this kind in the present Russian and German mentality. An outbreak of violent desires and impossible fantasies among the lower strata of the population is analogous to an outburst from the lower strata of the unconscious in an individual.[11]

In 1927 I expressed myself as follows:

The old religions with their sublime and ridiculous, their friendly and fiendish symbols did not drop from the blue, but were born of this human soul that dwells within us at this moment. All those things, in their primal forms, live on in us and may at any time burst in upon us with annihilating force, in the guise of mass-suggestions against which the individual is defenceless. Our fearsome gods have only changed their names: they now rhyme with -ism. Or has anyone the nerve to claim that the World War or Bolshevism was an ingenious invention? Just as outwardly we live in a world where a whole continent may be submerged at any moment, or a pole be shifted, or a new pestilence break out, so inwardly we live in a world where at any moment something similar may occur, albeit in the form of an idea, but no less dangerous and untrustworthy for that. Failure to adapt to this inner world is a negligence entailing just as serious consequences as ignorance and ineptitude in the outer world. It is after all only a tiny fraction of humanity, living mainly on that thickly populated peninsula of Asia which juts out into the Atlantic Ocean, and calling themselves "cultured," who, because they lack all contact with nature, have hit upon the idea that religion is a peculiar kind of mental disturbance of undiscoverable purport. Viewed from a safe distance, say from central Africa or Tibet, it would certainly look as if this fraction had projected its own unconscious mental derangements upon nations still possessed of healthy instincts.[12]

[10] *Two Essays*, par. 150; cf. *Collected Papers*, p. 432.

[11] "The Psychological Foundations of Belief in Spirits," reprinted in *Contributions to Analytical Psychology* (1928), pp. 265f. In *Über die Energetik der Seele* (1928) the end of this passage was revised as follows: ". . . the mental state of the people as a whole might well be compared to a psychosis," [Cf. *The Structure and Dynamics of the Psyche*, par. 595.—EDITORS.] [12] *Two Essays*, par. 326.

In 1928 I wrote that "the normal person . . . acts out his psychic disturbances socially and politically, in the form of mass psychoses like wars and revolutions."[13] A year later, in *The Secret of the Golden Flower*, which I published in collaboration with Richard Wilhelm, I remarked:

If we deny the existence of the autonomous systems, . . . they become an inexplicable source of disturbance which we finally assume must exist somewhere outside ourselves. The resultant projection creates a dangerous situation in that the disturbing effects are now attributed to a wicked will outside ourselves, which is naturally not to be found anywhere but with our neighbor *de l'autre côté de la rivière*. This leads to collective delusions, "incidents," revolutions, war—in a word, to destructive mass psychoses.[14]

In November 1932, the year in which Germany's fate was decided, I gave a lecture at the Austrian *Kulturbund* in Vienna, from which I should like to quote the following passage:

The gigantic catastrophes that threaten us today are not elemental happenings of a physical or biological order, but psychic events. To a quite terrifying degree we are threatened by wars and revolutions which are nothing other than psychic epidemics. At any moment several millions of human beings may be smitten with a new madness, and then we shall have another world war or devastating revolution. Instead of being at the mercy of wild beasts, earthquakes, landslides, and inundations, modern man is battered by the elemental forces of his own psyche. This is the World Power that vastly exceeds all other powers on earth. The Age of Enlightenment, which stripped nature and human institutions of gods, overlooked the God of Terror who dwells in the human soul. If anywhere, fear of God is justified in face of the overwhelming supremacy of the psychic.

But all this is so much abstraction. Everyone knows that the intellect, that clever jackanapes, can put it this way or any other way he pleases. It is a very different thing when the psyche, as an objective fact, hard as granite and heavy as lead, confronts a man as an inner experience and addresses him in an audible voice, saying, "This is what will and must be." Then he feels himself called, just as the group does when there's a war on, or a revolution, or any other madness. It is not for nothing that our age cries out for the redeemer personality, for the one who can emancipate himself from the grip of the collec-

[13] "General Aspects of Dream Psychology," in *The Structure and Dynamics of the Psyche*, par. 518.

[14] *Alchemical Studies*, par. 52.

tive and save at least his own soul, who lights a beacon of hope for others, proclaiming that here is at least *one* man who has succeeded in extricating himself from that fatal identity with the group psyche. For the group, because of its unconsciousness, has no freedom of choice, and so psychic activity runs on in it like an uncontrolled force of nature. There is thus set going a chain reaction that comes to a stop only in catastrophe. The people always long for a hero, a slayer of dragons, when they feel the danger of psychic forces; hence the cry for personality.[15]

There is no need to burden the reader with further quotations. Of course I never imagined that such observations would have an effect on any large scale, but it certainly never occurred to me that a time would come when I should be reproached for having said absolutely nothing about these things before 1945, that is, before my article "After the Catastrophe." When Hitler seized power it became quite evident to me that a mass psychosis was boiling up in Germany. But I could not help telling myself that this was after all Germany, a civilized European nation with a sense of morality and discipline. Hence the ultimate outcome of this unmistakable mass movement still seemed to me uncertain, just as the figure of the Führer at first struck me as being merely ambivalent. It is true that in July 1933, when I gave a series of lectures in Berlin, I received an extremely unfavourable impression both of the behaviour of the Party and of the person of Goebbels. But I did not wish to assume from the start that these symptoms were decisive, for I knew other people of unquestionable idealism who sought to prove to me that these things were unavoidable abuses such as are customary in any great revolution. It was indeed not at all easy for a foreigner to form a clear judgment at that time. Like many of my contemporaries, I had my doubts.

As a psychiatrist, accustomed to dealing with patients who are in danger of being overwhelmed by unconscious contents, I knew that it is of the utmost importance, from the therapeutic point of view, to strengthen as far as possible their conscious position and powers of understanding, so that something is there to intercept and integrate the contents that are breaking through into consciousness. These contents are not necessarily

---

[15] *The Development of the Personality, Coll. Works*, Vol. 17, pars. 302f.

destructive in themselves, but are ambivalent, and it depends entirely on the constitution of the intercepting consciousness whether they will turn out to be a curse or a blessing.

National Socialism was one of those psychological mass phenomena, one of those outbreaks of the collective unconscious, about which I had been speaking for nearly twenty years. The driving forces of a psychological mass movement are essentially archetypal. Every archetype contains the lowest and the highest, evil and good, and is therefore capable of producing diametrically opposite results. Hence it is impossible to make out at the start whether it will prove to be positive or negative. My medical attitude towards such things counselled me to wait, for it is an attitude that allows no hasty judgments, does not always know from the start what is better, and is willing to give things "a fair trial." Far from wishing to give the beleaguered consciousness its death-blow, it tries to strengthen its powers of resistance through insight, so that the evil that is hidden in every archetype shall not seize hold of the individual and drag him to destruction. The therapist's aim is to bring the positive, valuable, and living quality of the archetype—which will sooner or later be integrated into consciousness in any case—into reality, and at the same time to obstruct as far as possible its damaging and pernicious tendencies. It is part of the doctor's professional equipment to be able to summon up a certain amount of optimism even in the most unlikely circumstances, with a view to saving everything that it is still possible to save. He cannot afford to let himself be too much impressed by the real or apparent hopelessness of a situation, even if this means exposing himself to danger. Moreover, it should not be forgotten that Germany, up till the National Socialist era, was one of the most differentiated and highly civilized countries on earth, besides being, for us Swiss, a spiritual background to which we were bound by ties of blood, language, and friendship. I wanted to do everything within my feeble powers to prevent this cultural bond from being broken, for culture is our only weapon against the fearful danger of mass-mindedness.

If an archetype is not brought into reality consciously, there is no guarantee whatever that it will be realized in its favourable form; on the contrary, there is all the more danger of a destructive regression. It seems as if the psyche were endowed

84

with consciousness for the very purpose of preventing such destructive possibilities from happening.

Coming back to the question of "German psychopathy," I am as convinced as ever that National Socialism was the mass psychosis of which I have been speaking for so long. What happened in Germany can be explained, in my view, only by the existence of an abnormal state of mind. But I am open to conviction if anyone can prove to me that the phenomenology of National Socialism belongs to the normal inventory of the psyche. In Italy the mass psychosis took a somewhat milder form. Russia can plead, by way of excuse, the low level of popular education before the Revolution. But Germany was supposed to be a highly civilized country, and yet the horrors there exceeded anything the world has ever known. I therefore maintain that there are peculiar depths in the Germans which present the most violent contrast to their former high achievements. Such a condition is known in psychopathology as a dissociation, and a habitual dissociation is one of the signs of a psychopathic disposition.[16]

I am aware that the word "psychopathic" strikes harshly on the layman's ear, and that it conjures up all manner of horrors, such as lunatic asylums and the like. By way of explanation I should like to state that only a very small fraction of so-called psychopaths land in the asylum. The overwhelming majority of them constitute that part of the population which is alleged to be "normal." The concept of "normality" is an ideal construction. In psychology we speak of the "scope of the normal," thus implicitly admitting that the concept of normality swings between certain limits and cannot therefore be sharply defined. A rather bigger swing, and the psychic process has already entered the sphere of the abnormal. These deviations from the "norm" —and they are very common—pass unnoticed so long as they do not lead to actual signs of disease. But if definite and unmistakable symptoms occur, such as are obvious even to the layman, then the case is clearly "psychopathic" (i.e., a "suffering"— πάσχειν—of the psyche). The milder forms of psychopathy are the commonest and severe cases are rare. There are countless people who go a little bit beyond the scope of the normal, in one way

[16] For the necessary qualifications of this general statement see "After the Catastrophe," Chapter 5, pp. 62 and 63.

or another, either temporarily or chronically. If they get together in large numbers—which is what happens in any crowd—
abnormal phenomena appear. One need only read what Le
Bon[17] has to say on the "psychology of crowds" to understand
what I mean: man as a particle in the mass is psychically abnormal. Ignorance of this fact is no protection against it.

So anyone whose ears are offended by the word "psychopathic" is at liberty to suggest a soft, soothing, comforting sub-
stitute which correctly reflects the state of mind that gave birth
to National Socialism. Far from wishing to insult the German
people, my object, as I have said, is to diagnose the suffering
that has its roots in their psyche and is the cause of their downfall. Nothing will ever persuade me that Nazism was forced on
the German people by the Freemasons, the Jews, or the wicked
English—that is really too childish. I have heard that sort of
thing too often in the asylum.

Anyone who wishes to get a vivid picture of the workings of
psychopathic inferiority has only to study the way in which responsible Germans—i.e., the educated classes—react to the notorious *faits et gestes*. There is no doubt that a very large number of
Germans are chiefly annoyed at having lost the war. A large proportion of them are shocked that the regime of the occupying
forces is, in places, harsh, unjust, and even brutal—"after all,
the war's over now." They refuse to listen to the accounts of
Germany's unspeakable behaviour in Bohemia, Poland, Russia,
Greece, Holland, Belgium, Norway, and France. "All kinds of
regrettable things did happen, of course, but that was during
the war." A slightly larger number admit the concentration
camps and the "bad behaviour" in Poland and elsewhere, but
in the same breath begin to enumerate the outrages committed
by the English, from the Boer War on, without of course mentioning the war launched by their other psychopath, Wilhelm II.
It never seems to occur to them that someone else's sin in no
way excuses their own, and that their habit of accusing others
merely shows up their own lack of insight.

Finally we come to a smaller number—the better men of the
nation—who confess: *Pater, peccavi in caelum et coram te*, "we

---

[17] *The Crowd: A Study of the Popular Mind.* Cf. also Reinwald's *Vom Geist der Massen*, which
has just appeared [1946].

86

have our share of guilt in the desolation that has spread over the world. We know that we must bear the consequences of a war begun in a spirit of wantonness and criminality, and we would not think of trying to escape our hard fate, *not even by complaints and accusations*." [18] Such a confession can only be answered in the words of the evangelist: "Bring forth the best robe, and put it on him; and put a ring on his hand, and shoes on his feet; and bring hither the fatted calf, and kill it; and let us eat, and be merry: For this my son was dead, and is alive again." [19] It makes us feel something of the joy that reigned in heaven over the repentant sinner, and of the discomfiture of the ninety and nine just persons.

Yet what meets our eye in the very next sentence? "Nevertheless, as people who have declared themselves openly and with honest conviction, as Evangelical Christians, we should and must . . . point out with due emphasis that, according to the Gospel, no one is in greater danger than he who, *secure in the consciousness of his own innocence, judges and condemns another. . . .* We cannot, indeed we should not pass over in silence the fact that foreign statesmen and their governments also played a decisive part in that first European catastrophe, through their politics both before and after 1918, *which were likewise power-politics based on injustice,* and that, consequently, they contributed their share to the inflation and the economic crisis, to the impoverishment of the German nation, *and thus prepared the ground for the dragon's teeth from which National Socialism sprang up.*"

In the first passage we read that no one has any intention of accusing anybody, and in the second comes the accusation. The contradiction passes unnoticed. When confession and repentance are followed by an aggressive defence, the genuineness of the repentance becomes doubtful. As it is hardly credible that the authors of this document consciously set out to sabotage the effect of their confession, we can only conclude—as is unfortunately only too true in innumerable instances where similar arguments are put forward—that there is an astounding uncon-

[18] My italics. Here I am making use of an authentic document, the authors of which I do not wish to expose by name, as they are worthy people whose shortcomings are not a personal fault but a national one.
[19] Luke 15:22f.

sciousness of the fatal impression that such an attitude is bound to create.

Furthermore we must ask: Has Germany openly admitted that she is conscious of her guilt, if she now "judges and condemns" others? It seems to have escaped the notice of the authors that there are plenty of people in Europe who are capable of forming their own judgment, and who are not hoodwinked by such unconscious naïvetés. Thus our document turns into a rather indiscreet monologue thoroughly in keeping with the clinical picture. Parents and teachers, judges and psychiatrists, are well acquainted with this mixture of repentance and lust for revenge, this same unconsciousness and indifference to the disastrous impression one makes, this same self-centred disregard of one's fellow men. Such an attitude defeats its object: it sets out to evoke an impression of repentance, and the next minute it defends itself by launching an attack. This manoeuvre simply makes the repentance unreal and the defence ineffectual. It is too unconscious to serve any purpose, quite unadapted and not equal to the demands of reality. There is an old saying that goes: "Sickness is diminished adaptation." The kind of adaptation here illustrated is of no value either morally or intellectually; it is inferior, and psychopathically inferior at that.

In saying this it is not my intention to accuse or condemn. I am obliged to mention it only because my diagnosis has been doubted.[20] A medical diagnosis is not an accusation, and an illness is not a disgrace but a misfortune. As early as 1936 I pleaded for compassion in judging the German mentality.[21] Even now I adopt the standpoint of the therapist, and therefore, in the interests of the patient, I must emphasize the necessity for complete insight without any extenuating provisos. It avails him nothing to cultivate only a half-consciousness of his condition, and to cover up his other half with illusions whose colossal dangers he has just experienced in the most terrible form. My sympathy with the lot of the Germans is great, and I am only too painfully aware that my chances of being able to help are exceedingly small. I can only hope and pray that one of the worst

[20] Nor does my diagnosis include every individual German. I have heard statements from Germans which were spoken like a man and were not vitiated by that infantile weakness which underlies the German *Kraftmeier* style.

[21] Cf. "Wotan," supra, p. 22.

dangers now threatening Germany, besides economic distress, may soon some to an end, and that is her spiritual isolation. National isolation combined with mass psychology and centralization are Germany's bane. The task she has to fulfil is not political but spiritual, and the gifts she possesses for this are practically unique. We should therefore help and support this side of her nature by all the means within our power.

*

I cannot bring this epilogue to a close without saying a few words about the outlook for the future. No nation has ever fallen so low as the Germans and none has ever branded itself with such a stigma, which generations will not be able to wash away. But when a pendulum swings so violently in one direction, it is capable of swinging just as far in the other—if we may apply this analogy to the psyche of a nation. I do not know whether it is justified from the ethnopsychological point of view. I only know that, in the psyche of an individual with a tendency to dissociation, there can be violent oscillations, with the result that one extreme necessarily leads to its opposite. Provided, however, that he remains in full possession of his human qualities and thus has a mean value, I am inclined to think that the minus is balanced by the plus. In other words, I believe there is a faculty for regeneration in the Germans that might be able to find the right answer to the terrific tension between the opposites which has been so evident during the past twelve years. In this endeavour Germany would not be isolated, for all the positive spiritual forces which are at work throughout the civilized world would stand by her and sustain her effort. The struggle between light and darkness has broken out everywhere. The rift runs through the whole globe, and the fire that set Germany ablaze is smouldering and glowing wherever we look. The conflagration that broke out in Germany was the outcome of psychic conditions that are universal. The real danger signal is not the fiery sign that hung over Germany, but the unleashing of atomic energy, which has given the human race the power to annihilate itself completely. The situation is about the same as if a small boy of six had been given a bag of dynamite for a birthday present. We are not one hundred per cent convinced by his assurances that no calamity will happen. Will man be able to give up toying with the idea of another war? Can we at last get

89

it into our heads that any government of impassioned patriots which signs the order for mobilization should immediately be executed *en bloc*?

How can we save the child from the dynamite which no one can take away from him? The good spirit of humanity is challenged as never before. The facts can no longer be hushed up or painted in rosy colours. Will this knowledge inspire us to a great inner transformation of mind, to a higher, maturer consciousness and sense of responsibility?

It is time, high time, that civilized man turned his mind to fundamental things. It is now a question of existence or non-existence, and surely this should be subjected to the most searching investigation and discussion. For the danger that threatens us now is of such dimensions as to make this last European catastrophe seem like a curtain-raiser.

INDEX

THE COLLECTED WORKS OF
C. G. JUNG

T HE PUBLICATION of the first complete edition, in English, of the works of C. G. Jung was undertaken by Routledge and Kegan Paul, Ltd., in England and by Bollingen Foundation in the United States. The American edition is number XX in Bollingen Series, which since 1967 has been published by Princeton University Press. The edition contains revised versions of works previously published, such as *Psychology of the Unconscious*, which is now entitled *Symbols of Transformation*; works originally written in English, such as *Psychology and Religion*; works not previously translated, such as *Aion*; and, in general, new translations of virtually all of Professor Jung's writings. Prior to his death, in 1961, the author supervised the textual revision, which in some cases is extensive. Sir Herbert Read (d. 1968), Dr. Michael Fordham, and Dr. Gerhard Adler (d. 1988) compose the Editorial Committee; the translator is R. F. C. Hull (except for Volume 2) and William McGuire is executive editor.

The price of the volumes varies according to size; they are sold separately, and may also be obtained on standing order. Several of the volumes are extensively illustrated. Each volume contains an index and, in most cases, a bibliography; the final volumes contain a complete bibliography of Professor Jung's writings and a general index to the entire edition.

In the following list, dates of original publication are given in parentheses (of original composition, in brackets). Multiple dates indicate revisions.

*1. PSYCHIATRIC STUDIES

On the Psychology and Pathology of So-Called Occult Phenomena (1902)

On Hysterical Misreading (1904)

Cryptomnesia (1905)

On Manic Mood Disorder (1903)

A Case of Hysterical Stupor in a Prisoner in Detention (1902)

On Simulated Insanity (1903)

A Medical Opinion on a Case of Simulated Insanity (1904)

A Third and Final Opinion on Two Contradictory Psychiatric Diagnoses (1906)

On the Psychological Diagnosis of Facts (1905)

†2. EXPERIMENTAL RESEARCHES

Translated by Leopold Stein in collaboration with Diana Riviere

STUDIES IN WORD ASSOCIATION (1904–7, 1910)

The Associations of Normal Subjects (by Jung and F. Riklin)

An Analysis of the Associations of an Epileptic

The Reaction-Time Ratio in the Association Experiment

Experimental Observations on the Faculty of Memory

Psychoanalysis and Association Experiments

The Psychological Diagnosis of Evidence

Association, Dream, and Hysterical Symptom

The Psychopathological Significance of the Association Experiment

Disturbances in Reproduction in the Association Experiment

The Association Method

The Family Constellation

PSYCHOPHYSICAL RESEARCHES (1907–8)

On the Psychophysical Relations of the Association Experiment

Psychophysical Investigations with the Galvanometer and Pneumograph in Normal and Insane Individuals (by F. Peterson and Jung)

Further Investigations on the Galvanic Phenomenon and Respiration in Normal and Insane Individuals (by C. Ricksher and Jung)

Appendix: Statistical Details of Enlistment (1906); New Aspects of Criminal Psychology (1908); The Psychological Methods of Investigation Used in the Psychiatric Clinic of the University of Zurich (1910); On the Doctrine of Complexes ([1911] 1913); On the Psychological Diagnosis of Evidence (1937)

* Published 1957; 2nd edn., 1970.　　　　　+ Published 1973.

* Published 1960.   † Published 1961.
‡ Published 1956; 2nd edn., 1967. (65 plates, 43 text figures.)

* Published 1971.   † Published 1953; 2nd edn., 1966.
‡ Published 1960; 2nd edn., 1969.

Psychological Factors Determining Human Behavior (1937)
Instinct and the Unconscious (1919)
The Structure of the Psyche (1927/1931)
On the Nature of the Psyche (1947/1954)
General Aspects of Dream Psychology (1916/1948)
On the Nature of Dreams (1945/1948)
The Psychological Foundations of Belief in Spirits (1920/1948)
Spirit and Life (1926)
Basic Postulates of Analytical Psychology (1931)
Analytical Psychology and *Weltanschauung* (1928/1931)
The Real and the Surreal (1933)
The Stages of Life (1930–1931)
The Soul and Death (1934)
Synchronicity: An Acausal Connecting Principle (1952)
Appendix: On Synchronicity (1951)

*9. PART I. THE ARCHETYPES AND THE
COLLECTIVE UNCONSCIOUS
Archetypes of the Collective Unconscious (1934/1954)
The Concept of the Collective Unconscious (1936)
Concerning the Archetypes, with Special Reference to the Anima
    Concept (1936/1954)
Psychological Aspects of the Mother Archetype (1938/1954)
Concerning Rebirth (1940/1950)
The Psychology of the Child Archetype (1940)
The Psychological Aspects of the Kore (1941)
The Phenomenology of the Spirit in Fairytales (1945/1948)
On the Psychology of the Trickster-Figure (1954)
Conscious, Unconscious, and Individuation (1939)
A Study in the Process of Individuation (1934/1950)
Concerning Mandala Symbolism (1950)
Appendix: Mandalas (1955)

*9. PART II. AION (1951)
    RESEARCHES INTO THE PHENOMENOLOGY OF THE SELF
The Ego
The Shadow
The Syzygy: Anima and Animus
The Self
Christ, a Symbol of the Self
The Sign of the Fishes   (*continued*)

* Published 1959; 2nd edn., 1968. (Part I: 79 plates, with 29 in colour.)

* Published 1964; 2nd edn., 1970. (8 plates.)
† Published 1958; 2nd edn., 1969.

* Published 1953; 2nd edn., completely revised, 1968. (270 illustrations.)
† Published 1968. (50 plates, 4 text figures.)
‡ Published 1963; 2nd edn., 1970. (10 plates.)

* Published 1966.
† Published 1954; 2nd edn., revised and augmented, 1966. (13 illustrations.)
‡ Published 1954.

The Development of Personality (1934)
Marriage as a Psychological Relationship (1925)

*18. THE SYMBOLIC LIFE
Miscellaneous writings

†19. COMPLETE BIBLIOGRAPHY OF C. G. JUNG'S WRITINGS

‡20. GENERAL INDEX TO THE COLLECTED WORKS

§ THE ZOFINGIA LECTURES
Supplementary Volume A to The Collected Works Edited by William
McGuire, translated by Jan van Heurck, introduction by Marie-Louise
von Franz

Related publications:
C. G. JUNG: LETTERS
Selected and edited by Gerhard Adler, in collaboration with Aniela Jaffé.
Translations from the German by R. F. C. Hull.
VOL. 1: 1906-1950
VOL. 2: 1951-1961

C. G. JUNG SPEAKING: Interviews and Encounters
Edited by William McGuire and R. F. C. Hull

C. G. JUNG: Word and Image
Edited by Aniela Jaffé

THE ESSENTIAL JUNG
Selected and introduced by Anthony Storr

Notes of C. G. Jung's Seminars:

‖ DREAM ANALYSIS (1928-1930)
Edited by William McGuire

NIETZSCHE'S *ZARATHUSTRA* (1934-1939)
Edited by James L. Jarrett (2 vols.)

**ANALYTICAL PSYCHOLOGY (1925)
Edited by William McGuire

CHILDREN'S DREAMS (1936-1941)
Edited by Lorenz Jung

* Published 1954.	‖ Published 1984.
† Published 1976.	# Published 1988.
‡ Published 1979.	**Published 1989.
§ Published 1983.	